DATE			

TWO FOR THE SHOW
Great Comedy Teams

GEORGE: Which came first, the chicken or the egg?
GRACIE: I didn't even know they were here. I better go to the store.

This was a typical exchange between the comedy team of Burns and Allen. The jokes as well as the stories behind the people who told them are presented in this look at comedy teams. Amos 'n' Andy, Laurel and Hardy, and Abbott and Costello are all classics in the field. You will also learn about the origins of Rowan and Martin's "Laugh In" and the censorship battle that finally drove the Smothers Brothers off television. Everything from early vaudeville to "Saturday Night Live" and Cheech and Chong is included in this book about the teams that make people laugh.

GREAT COMEDY TEAMS

TWO FOR THE SHOW

Lonnie Burr

PHOTOGRAPHS

JULIAN MESSNER
NEW YORK

For Groucho Marx, whom I did not know personally.

For Joe Smith, of Smith & Dale, whom I know only tangentially.

For Diane Dickey, without whose encouragement in this project I would have impaled myself on a rubber spatula, and without whose research assistance this tome would have been a three-page tome . . .

And without whom there is very little in the world. ARA VOS PREC.

Copyright © 1979 by Lonnie Burr
Second Printing, 1979
All rights reserved
including the right of reproduction
in whole or in part in any form
Published by Julian Messner
A Simon & Schuster Division of
Gulf & Western Corporation
Simon & Schuster Building
1230 Avenue of the Americas
New York, New York 10020

Designed by Irving Perkins
Manufactured in the United States of America

Library of Congress Cataloging in Publication Data

Burr, Lonnie.
  Two for the show.

  Bibliography: p.
  Includes index.
  1. Comedy shows—United States—Juvenile literature.   2. Comedy
films—United States—Juvenile literature.   I. Title.
PN1991.8.C65B8   791.43′028′0922   78–31674
ISBN 0–671–32915–4

Contents

A Note from Stiller and Meara

My first comedy partner was a dog. His name was Crab, and he appeared with me in Joseph Papp's production of "Two Gentlemen of Verona" in the late 50s. Crab had no special breed but was a cur of the highest order. I called him a Shakespearian Retriever in honor of every laugh I missed and he saved.

There is a comfort and warmth when you're basking in an audience's laughter on the stage like bathing in a sea of acceptance. Someone actually had the temerity to say, "Mr. Stiller, by thy dog thou shalt be known." Taking second billing didn't bother me compared to the joy of acting with this noble canine.

By this time Crab was no longer my stage partner, but a permanent live-in member of our household. He had taken over. My affection for him was threatening my marriage. Anne was about to name him as a correspondent in a divorce action. She was right—I couldn't let go!

Those loving nights on stage in Central Park were still haunting me. Now I understood Paddy Chayefskey's "Marty/Angie" relationship.

To save my marriage I jokingly suggested that Anne might like working on a comedy act. Grasping at any straw that would keep the flame of our love a flicker, she said, "Yes." That decision changed my life! Having a human partner is very warm and comforting. It was even more comforting to work with Anne, my wife, than with Crab.

We were never competitive. I never resented her laughs because we were sharing and trusting and she was funnier. The basis of all great teamwork is trust. When you have it, you can reach levels you never dreamed you could reach. Essentially it is Anne's honesty that makes her funny. She is also pretty, rather unusual for most comediennes who trade on putting themselves down for flaws we all have anyway.

We have been told that one of our assets is timing. It is hard for me to explain how you develop that sense of timing, but it is important not to have preconceived ideas as to what's funny.

Also important is the trip on the way. We try to enjoy it.

Pain is pain. We all experience it in getting to what finally works. Working one-on-one comedically has its bruising moments, but we have a rule, "If I criticize your comedy choices, I am not criticizing your intelligence or your manhood. I still love you."

It was luck and the G.I. Bill that got me to Syracuse University and Professors Sawyer Falk and Frederic Schweppe who gave me the chance to learn in front of people—their support was open-ended.

I first learned about endowing an audience with an identity from Walt Witcover, a friend and teacher who shared all his secrets about how an actor must play with his audience. His joy of the craft made working with him something special. Anne and I improvised our first routine, "Jonah," a man swallowed by a whale in Miami Beach, in Witcover's presence.

Anne never went to college. She does everything quite intuitively. Perhaps it was the influence of Alfred Linder, a fine teacher who always told Anne, "You're very talented but you don't work hard enough." Alfred was only half right. Anne works very hard, but like all such gifted people, her creativity seems effortless.

There are no rules about what makes a comedy team work, but it takes a great deal of strength, understanding, fight, trust, and the ability to give in and respect one another.

Jerry Stiller

P.S. "A dog's life with Jerry Stiller isn't too bad!"

Anne Meara

Introduction

In the beginning, there was a stand-up comic. But he was not alone for long.

A caveman jumped up after his meal one night and told his family and friends about the perils that he had encountered during his daily search for food. Thus, theater was born. It is quite likely that formal comedy was born then, too. It doesn't take much of a strain on the imagination to suspect that after scrounging the hinterlands for food all day, meeting constant dangers along the way, a person would like to laugh. A person needed to laugh.

After the caveman got his first laugh, he most likely went for more laughs. People like to laugh. Even more, people like to make other people laugh.

GRONK: So I went up to where the pterodactyl was lying and clubbed him in the shin. He didn't . . .
GRINK: Why in the shin?
GRONK: . . . Uh . . . it's a shin to pterodactyl lie.
   (Cave people groans and laughter)
GRINK: Why didn't you just use a spear?
GRONK: Because, dummy, I belong to a Hunting Club.

It was corny, sure, but it certainly brightened up the dull nights at Cave 666. Grink, interrupting and asking questions, has become a straight man to Gronk. And he has led us to the first comedy team.

Civilized humans have been trying to analyze and define comedy since the beginning of recorded time. No one has succeeded. All we do know is that people have always laughed. And wherever or whenever there is one person who laughs, there are one or more persons trying to make people laugh. Comedy developed formally in various literary forms: epic poems, plays, satires, and so on. These usually involved dialogue and, hence, two or more people exchanging words. If Thespis was the first actor, coming out of the Greek chorus to speak alone, the first official comedian was the court jester, an actor-author whose job was literally in constant jeopardy. But as long as there have been verbal exchanges, there have been comedy teams.

This book is not intended to be a comprehensive study of every comedy team that has existed. There are numerous books that cover many of the better-known teams in much more detail. What this book does do is try to give a through line to comedy teams and their development from the beginning of the twentieth century until the present: 1978. The teams included have all proved themselves in one way or another. The early vaudeville teams are too numerous to cover thoroughly, but the ones that have lasted are touched on. Teams that were not really teams or were teams for a short time, such as Percy Kilbride and Marjorie Main in the *Ma and Pa Kettle* films, have been excluded for the most part. There is a definite emphasis on the teams that have come to the fore in the last twenty years, the teams that have had no books written about them.

I have attempted to ascertain the facts and/or the truth about all the teams included, which is not an easy feat since there are usually at least two or more contradictory versions, sometimes even when the party discussed is still alive. A Glossary is provided at the back of the book so that words or phrases such as "talking woman" or "olio" will not confound the reader. There is also a Chronology following the

Glossary that traces the lives and events of the major comedy teams from 1898 to 1978.

Numerous kind folks have helped in getting the facts and putting the book together. With special thanks to researcher Diane Dickey, those other helpful people are Dick Martin, Mae Woods, Jack Burns, Dick Clair, Natalie Goodman, Jack Langdon, Jenna McMahon, Marty Halperin, and Joe Smith.

I have tried to capture the texture of the various teams from Smith and Dale to Cheech and Chong. Although there are similarities between the two teams, there is quite a difference in texture. I have also attempted to make the bald facts as palatable as possible. Comedy, like love, is easier to experience than it is to describe. But a great deal of the fun is in the describing. I've had fun writing the book; I hope you have fun reading it.

Lonnie Burr

PART I
The
Old World

CHAPTER 1

Through Thick and Thin
(Laurel and Hardy)

Exterior. Two men walk up to the front door of a mansion. One man is fat and wears a too-tight coat, a snug-fitting derby and a tiny four-in-hand tie. The other man is skinny, his pants a little baggy, and he also wears a derby and a formal wing collar and tie. The skinny man starts to knock on the door but the fat man stops him, indicating that he must take off his hat. The skinny man does so and we see that his hair appears as if he has just stuck his finger in an electrical socket while bathing.

The skinny man knocks and the two men smile at each other. Nothing happens. He knocks again. He turns and smiles at the fat man, who is less amused. Nothing happens. The thin man, perplexed, starts to knock once more but the fat man, with a superior air, halts him and proceeds to demonstrate the proper form for knocking.

He elaborately prepares himself and begins to knock with a flourish of his hand. He knowingly glances at his friend. The door opens and he continues to knock on the chest of a very large butler.

Realizing something is wrong, he turns to confront the odd-sounding door. He quickly pushes the skinny man in front and hides his chagrin. The skinny man innocently stares at the huge, glaring butler and begins to cry, playing with his porcupine hair as a child would.

The butler pats him on the shoulder and steps aside to admit him. The fat man nudges the thin man, acknowledging his expertise. The thin man enters and the door is shut. The fat man runs into the door nose first. After indulging his pain and checking for fracture, the fat man stares at us resignedly.

The door opens and the skinny man is thrown out. He runs into the fat man and both fall to the ground. They exchange a few shoves, shrug, and then help each other up. Reconciled, they continue on their way.

The beginning for Arthur Stanley Jefferson and Oliver Norvell Hardy was slightly different, but the ending was the same. They continue on their way, reconciled, a unit, a team.

Stan Laurel was born in Lancashire, England; Oliver ("Babe") Hardy in Harlem, Georgia. Stan was skinny, Ollie was fat. Stan was a music hall comedian (the English counterpart of vaudeville), Ollie was a villain in two-reeler silent movies. How they got together and became America's most famous and idolized comedy team is a little like the scene described above.

Both boys grew up with a common dislike of school and a flair for entertaining—Ollie as the class clown and Stan as an extension of his performing environment. Stan was around theaters constantly, for his father, A. J. (Arthur Jefferson), had given up a career as an entertainer to manage theatricals. Stan made his first appearance before an audience in 1905 at age sixteen. He then continued to learn his craft in England and Scotland, safe from the tedium of the classroom. Oliver, born in 1892 and two years younger than Stanley, actually beat his future partner by running away to join "Coburn's Minstrels" at the age of eight. But Ollie returned to a more normal life after this short experience and didn't venture further on the stage, except for school revues and impromptu fooling, until 1913. Then, in his twenty-first year, he traveled to Jacksonville, Florida, to be in the moving pictures. He had started the first movie theater in Milledgeville, Georgia, in 1910 and finally decided that what he was seeing on the screen was something he could do just as well as anyone else.

Stan fought harder. He left school, after many earlier attempts, to work in the box office for his dad. He watched the acts at the theater and copied them until he felt he was ready to try it on his own at Pickard's Theatre in Glasgow, Scotland. The act was a combination of eccentric dancing, some singing, and some physical humor. The appearance was successful enough to encourage him to continue. His first professional job was in 1907 in an English touring company of *Sleeping Beauty*. Later he joined Fred Karno's show, *Mumming Birds*. Karno was famous in the history of British music hall for the perfection of his pantomimes. Besides rooming with the man he understudied, Charlie Chaplin, Stan learned the art of mime. In 1910 Karno's American version of *Mumming Birds—A Night in an English Music Hall* —toured the States and thus Stanley made his American debut.

It was not until 1917, after returning to England, changing his name from Stan Jefferson to Stan Laurel, and eventually finding a way back to the U.S., that he made his first two-reeler film for Adolph Ramish. Ramish owned the Hippodrome vaudeville house in Los Angeles, and seeing Stan do his act with his female partner convinced him that he could make money by discovering another Charlie Chaplin. Together they made a comedy entitled *Nuts in May* and after that there was no question that Stan would stay in America and pursue his career. Stan signed a contract at Universal Pictures as a result of his first two-reeler. He began doing films as Hickory Hiram, the pattern being to establish a character and then do sequels. After completing a few Hiram films, there was a shuffle at the studio and Stan was dropped once more on to the stage.

Stan Laurel in a typical pose while preparing spaghetti. (*Courtesy Janus Films Inc.*)

One year later he was involved with cinema again and from 1920 to 1926 he freelanced. He worked for Hal Roach, a famous producer, with Larry Semon, a comedian at Vitagraph Studios, and wrote and performed for "Bronco Billy" Anderson, a cowboy star from the early silents who had turned to producing. In 1918 Stan made a two-reeler for Anderson called *Lucky Dog* and worked with a comedy villain named Oliver Hardy. Neither of them had any thought of becoming part of a comedy team.

Although an ingrained Southerner, Oliver Norvell Hardy's background was English and Scottish. His father had been a lawyer, which prompted the boy to study law for a while after completing military school, but Mr. Hardy the elder died early and, similarly, Ollie lost his feeling for jurisprudence. He never lost his tenor voice which was quite good as a boy, hitting the sought-after high "C" easily and earning him praise. After joining Lubin Motion Pictures in Jacksonville for five dollars a day, he did some Billy West comedies in New York, tried Florida again, and finally came to California and the famous Vitagraph. It was while he was in Florida that he acquired his nickname "Babe." The name stuck with him throughout his life despite the fact that it originated as a casual title that his friends kidded him about.

Partially due to his size, somewhere around three hundred pounds when not on a diet, Ollie was inevitably cast as a heavy in the numerous comedies he filmed before teaming up with Stan. Heavies were the villains, the term deriving from the heavy make-up that the bad guys always wore: bushy eyebrows, mustaches, beards, and so on.

In 1926 Stan and Ollie became part of Hal Roach's stock players, a stable of actors who would weave in and out of various roles in any film that the producer made. Ollie was one of the resident heavies and Stan was a writer and sometimes director. By this time Stan was making quite a name for himself by doing parodies of other films. Before teaming up with Ollie he had approximately sixty "shorts" (the term for one- and two-reel films that ran from ten to twenty minutes) in the can (completed). In minor roles, Ollie must have had more, since he had been making films longer than Stan. Neither one would make a full-length feature until the 1930s. Stan's satires can be indicated by their titles: *Rob 'Em Good*, jibing *Robin Hood; Mud and Sand*, poking fun at matinee idol Rudolph Valentino's famous *Blood and Sand;* and many others, including *Wild Bill Hiccup* and *Dr. Pyckle and Mr. Pryde.* But Stan the writer and Oliver the villain were still not matched.

Roach was making a series of films that capitalized on stars, such as Theda Bara, who were no longer at the peak of their careers. Thus, the producer got a big name for little money and the stars, already in trouble, got a chance for some new life. Stan, who began to prefer work behind the camera, was directing one of these vehicles when Babe had an accident. Stan was persuaded to take over the role for Babe and Roach, seeing a good thing, coaxed Stan to come from behind the camera to play in front of it once more. This led to Laurel and Hardy appearing together in *Slipping Wives*. But it wasn't until *Putting Pants on Philip* that the two comedians officially worked together as a team, and that team was still not the one we all recognize now as Laurel and Hardy. The two distinct characters had not yet developed. It also took a little while before the wide appeal of these two dignified buffoons dawned on Hal Roach as a salable commodity. Two years later, in 1928, they were established as a comedy team and began to resemble the two lovable fools that still light up screens all over the world.

The finalizing of the two characters, Mr. Hardy and Mr. Laurel, took place during the next few years at Roach. The derby was a standard comedic prop before Chaplin made it famous and Oliver had taken to using it during his Florida days. He started forming his "existence" based on Helpful Henry, a cartoon character of the time. Oliver always felt that the sight of an assured person making a fool of himself was much funnier than the sight of a fumble-bum fumbling. So he set about creating a man of taste who, on the surface, has complete control of his composure and his fate. The famous gesture of waving with both hands caught up in his four-in-hand tie whenever nervous, embarrassed, or apologetic, came by accidental improvisation in one of his early movies with Stan. The slow burn, Edgar Kennedy's specialty —a very slow, nonverbal way of expressing rage—was evolved into a direct burn into the camera in much the same improvisational fashion. His overly florid signature, prefaced with an exaggerated preparation, also became a part of the tasteful Mr. Hardy. Later, Art Carney would use a similar device for the character of Norton on "The Honeymooners" television series with Jackie Gleason.

Stan had studied mime in England. One of the most obvious and common features of mime artists is the highlighting of the face by blanking it out in one way or another and then accenting, much as a clown in a circus might. Stanley stated that he used light make-up and attempted to make his eyes tinier. He also rounded his eyebrows as a clown might. Babe had a different way of accenting; he combed his hair forward in an affected, flat pompadour and adopted a half-caterpillar mustache. Stan's crying, more or less his trademark, came to be a burden.

In *Get 'Em Young*, the early film (1926) in which Stan replaced Ollie, he played the role of an obsequious butler and, at one point, began bawling. This initiated the well-known crying of Laurel, the head-massaging gesture coming later. Unfortunately, Hal Roach was so taken with the bit that the minute he could find nothing else to do he would call on Stan to cry.

The famous haircut or *coiffure électrique*, was also an accident. Stan got a crew-cut for a prison film. He would put on a hat and his hair would stay in strange configurations. Everyone off-camera was so amused by the hair, he kept it. He started augmenting the effect by pulling his hair while scratching his head and, although he always did it when crying, he did it most any time after it became established.

As we see them, Stan and Ollie seem to dress rather oddly. Their outfits resemble those of somewhat shabby, down-and-out men servants. They did not think their costuming was particularly unusual, and definitely not outlandish. The costumes were meant to be formal—the dark suits, the stand-up collars, the derbies. Given the period in which they started

Stan Laurel (l.) and Oliver Hardy (r.) seated on couch in dentist's office (*Leave 'em Laughing*—Roach/MGM 1928). This was their third film as a team. (*Courtesy Janus Films Inc.*)

using them, the late twenties, they were not that bizarre. They tried to establish a sense of dignity, albeit a false dignity, that lent itself to puncturing. But it was not to be the freak look of a clown. To be sure, they were an odd-looking couple even in 1926, but there was a sense of reality to it all and, as Hardy has been quoted as saying, however wacky they were, they insisted on keeping a consistent sense of reality.

Another "bit" that developed improvisatorily during filming and which seems a logical outcome of their character is the precedence of Hardy the knowledgeable one. Ollie always precedes Stan, ostensibly due to his superior wisdom and, perhaps, due to his girth. Naturally it leads, more often than not, to hilarious disaster.

In all relationships involving two people, one of the persons is somewhat dominant. Ollie portrayed the more knowledgeable, polite, worldly one of the duo. He attempted to be proper, even elegant, at all times. His logic was at the forefront at all moments. Unfortunately, his logic was very bad and having it up front was an ill choice for Stan and Ollie, but a good choice for the viewer. Babe was larger and, seemingly, more powerful, so it was natural for him to take care of his friend. Stan was the smaller, the dependent one, the crybaby. Stanley, the innocent, always helpful in the wrong way, always doing the menial tasks like cooking or the dishes, took on the role of the simple country cousin. But he was so genuine in the role and so well meaning that you had to love him.

The working together of Stan and Ollie off-camera can be explained in the use of the slow burn take that Ollie had incorporated as one of the elements that established pace in film comedy. Oliver came upon the take almost by accident. From his writing and directing Stan had realized that a film audience had to be predicted. Unlike a live audience that you could wait for if their laughter stopped a scene or a bit, you had to give a film audience laughing space. The only way to do that was to allow for laughs at certain points without being obvious.

After being established as the top comedy draw in 1930, Laurel and Hardy faced their next obstacle: sound. Unlike the majority of Hollywood stars, Laurel and Hardy did not have a great amount of difficulty in making the transition. Their first two films were a little strained, but they soon became as adept in talkies as they had been in silents. First of all, their voices were in tune with their characters. Hardy was at home with his slightly affected, slightly exaggerated American Southern and Laurel was almost classic in coupling his timid scatterbrained character with the clipped, priggish (to American ears) English accent. Second, the universality of their humor was based on no language. Since the new humor would have to be a combination of both the visual and the auditory, verbal humor seemed to take over for most comedians. The majority of comics are still unknown outside their own country and language because of this obstacle. Stan and Ollie retained their visual humor intact as their staple and simply augmented it with good, simple comedy dialogue. The dialogue was usually an extension of what they did physically, which means that they were engaged in a series of non sequiturs, using a logic that would lead to false conclusions. So, instead of coming apart in fear of the new cinema, they realized that film was still basically a visual medium and, without panic, they utilized it fully.

STAN: Oh Ollie—You remember how dumb I used to be?
BABE: I certainly do!
STAN: Well, I'm better now.
BABE: I'm glad to hear it!

This exchange from *Block Heads* (1938) illustrates their sincere lack of sense. And from *Way Out West* (1936):

(Stan and Babe are lost.)
BABE: This is the way!
STAN: Uh, uh. It's this way.
BABE: Can't you read? We have to go the way that sign points.
  (The sign is being blown by the wind. There is no way to tell if it is accurate.)
BABE: Now we don't know which way to go.
STAN: Let's go this way.
BABE: Why should we go that way when it might be this way?
  (An Indian brave passes by. Stan speaks to him.)
STAN: Pardon me, mister, but which way is right?
  (The brave thinks for a second and then points to his right.)
STAN: You see, I was right. It's that way.
BABE: That's all I wanted to know.

Dialogue, although better than adequate in many of their films, was not what they are known and loved for. Many feel that their best films were the early movies that used a minimum of words. Their faultless timing in physical gags and bits is still a marvel to watch. Like all of the silent film stars, they were masters of mime.

In the changeover to sound films, Stan, as would be expected, happened onto the key of coordinating sound other than dialogue with physical business. The sound did not necessarily have to be true to life in this translation. Whether on stage, in film, or on the living room TV set, no one wants to see a person hurt. It is the experience of seeing someone fall or run into a door and knowing that it is only make-believe that makes it funny, as opposed to tragic. So, the delicacy of making something believable, like being hit by a two-ton truck, while not making it real, became a distinct problem. Now, with people actually talking in films, the audience accepted the convention as the reality. Stan prevented this by showing the person starting to fall down the stairs, then focusing on something else (for instance, a picture of someone watching the action) while the audience heard the person fall. Stan did not originate the device but he certainly contributed to its perfection. His was an innovative approach to the problem. In the same fashion he came up with false sounds for effects that were better than the actual sounds one might make accidentally when stepping on a cat or feasting on a pop bottle. The destructive element that had been a mainstay of early Chaplin and Keystone Kop films was made funnier in Laurel and Hardy scenarios by slowing down the violence and the consequent escalation, which built up suspense and anticipation. That is not to say that the film was reduced to slow motion; the action itself was interrupted by various elements and took more time to develop. The audience was allowed vicariously to enjoy the

peculiarly unreal violence of comedy without being sub-
jected to unnecessary brutality.

The next transition was the hardest to surmount and
proved, for various reasons, one that they were not capable
of conquering. Ollie and Stan made their first full-length
film, *Pardon Us*, in 1931. The previous silents had culmi-
nated in their one Academy Award for a short subject in
1932 (*The Music Box*). But with Hal Roach pursuing feature length films in order to keep abreast of the swiftly
changing movie business, Laurel and Hardy were forced
into making longer pictures. This involved them, as it did
the Marx Brothers, in the silliness and tedium of subplots—
usually the innocuous and boring young lovers—that put
huge gaps between their appearances and detracted from
the enjoyment of the team and, hence, the film. Stan felt
that their comedy could not sustain a full-length film. He
seemed right at the time but, in hindsight, he may have
made one of his rare errors in regard to film and comedy.
The problem was not with L & H but how to deal with the
gaps that their absence allowed and, without the help of
Irving Thalberg which the Marx Brothers had, the gaps were
not dealt with wisely.

The next difficulty was economic. Their contracts with
Roach were nearing an end and there was unrest on both
social and artistic levels. There were minimal successes with
features but things were not to everyone's liking. In 1940
Babe made *Zenobia* on his own for Roach, prompting rumors
about ill feelings between the two comics. The rumors were
unfounded. Babe was merely finishing out his contract with
Roach, Stan's having ended a year earlier. The partners attempted to start their own company but the company never
made a film. After going back to touring before live audiences, they returned to films after a two-year absence and
found it necessary to ally themselves first with 20th Century-
Fox and then MGM, which had released most of their films

Oliver "Babe" Hardy (l.) and Stan Laurel (r.) in the mid-1930s wearing the styles and expressions that made them famous. (*Courtesy Janus Films Inc.*)

with Roach. This marks the end, except for bits and pieces, of their best work. There are many reasons why they lost favor in the eyes of the public, one reason being the Marx Brothers' success with their madcap films. Roach, with whatever faults one wants to attribute to him, allowed L & H to do pretty much what they wanted to do. The all-knowing bigwigs at MGM and 20th would not. Stan and Ollie fought but it was made clear that they had to kowtow or be dropped. They elected, at least for a while, to tow the line.

From 1941 to 1945 they attempted to make their creatively hogtied situation work in films like *Jitterbugs*, *The Dancing Masters*, *The Bull Fighters*, and others. The films were only ghosts of their stronger work and so they began touring England and Europe with success. It was worthwhile to find that their adulation was worldwide, but there was still a need to do what they did best: make films. Their last cinematic effort, a joint European venture that allowed them less leeway than the moguls at 20th and MGM had provided, was finished in 1950. *Atoll K*, variously released in 1952 in the United States as *Robinson Crusoeland* and in England as *Utopia*, was a disaster. Stan became sick during the filming but they toured again in 1952 after his recovery. Two years later they returned home to what seemed like retirement.

Then, suddenly, in 1955 an echo from the past changed their status. Hal Roach, Jr., son of their old boss, began running Laurel and Hardy films on TV. They became stars all over again—if anything, bigger stars than before. The younger Roach planned to do some hour-long features with the two for TV but Babe Hardy became ill. The specials were scrapped. The illness was not new but he had concealed it previously. Now he lost over 110 pounds and never fully recovered. He died on August 7, 1957.

Stanley spent his remaining years with his wife in Santa Monica, California, being visited by worshipping comics and indulging himself by personally answering his voluminous fan mail. He was awarded a special Oscar for his contribution to comedy and never lost his gift for humor. According to comedian Dick Van Dyke, who portrayed Laurel in a 1978 television feature on the team, Stan even paraphrased the legendary quote on W. C. Fields' tombstone—"I'd rather be in Philadelphia." Van Dyke has related that one day, Stan, close to death, glibly commented to an attending nurse that, as opposed to being where he was, he would just as soon be skiing. Naturally, he had never been skiing. Stan Laurel died in February 1964.

The legacy of Stan and Babe is enormous. The films, even those marred by the studio's lack of taste or a flimsy subplot, are masterpieces that will continue to make viewers of any nationality laugh until people stop laughing. Like Chaplin, the two, individually and together, serve as a model for other comedians. There is no doubt that Abbott and Costello, Martin and Lewis, Dick Van Dyke, Red Skelton, Johnny Carson, and others have benefited from their example. There are also a few filmmakers who are in their debt: Woody Allen, Blake Edwards, Mel Brooks.

The mime of Stan has been an inspiration for Marcel Marceau, the physical comedy of Van Dyke, as well as the marvelous Inspector Clouseau character created by Peter Sellers in the *Pink Panther* films. The techniques of Stan and Ollie are facts that cannot be avoided by anyone involved in making people laugh. The use of sound in their talkies, the exploitation of the destructive nature in all of us, their improvisation, their attempt at social politesse (a mannerly way of making fools of ourselves), their faith in the visual element inherent in comedy, and the other tenets of their films cannot be ignored.

To try to single out one of their more than one hundred films as definitive would be presumptuous, not to mention impossible. For some it would be the 1932 Academy Award winning *The Music Box*. This short work is on the simple plot of a never-ending struggle to get a piano up some formidable stairs and into a house. They have to overcome numerous obstacles, not least of which is Billy Gilbert, and then, reaching the goal, they find that instead of solving a problem they have created one. Or *Two Tars* in 1928, with destruction becoming a hysterical metaphor for man's childishness and simple-mindedness. The back and forth of Stan and Ollie destroying Edgar Kennedy's car after a minor traffic accident, and Edgar's revenge—all in a slow, methodical fashion—can make anyone cry with anticipatory glee. Or the early *Battle of the Century* (1927), in which the pies from Mack Sennett's silents reached their classic height in a frothy carnage that has yet to be matched, though frequently tried. Others would vote for one of the full-length talkies: *Way Out West, Sons of the Desert* (the title being adopted by their fan club, which is quite active in 1978, just recently dedicating a gravesite to Hardy), *Babes in Toyland,* or *A Chump at Oxford,* the one film in which Stan was allowed to be superior to Ollie and did a wonderful job of it. There is no picking any one or two films from their many shorts and features. You be the judge.

Laurel and Hardy were a team from 1926 until 1955, but they are still a team and will always remain inextricably twined. At fourteen, Ollie was over 250 pounds and anxious to get a laugh. At sixteen, Stan was a little more than half that weight but just as anxious to "get on the halls," which was the English way of saying you wanted to be performing for an audience. Maybe their success was due to the fact that even a child could see their stupidity and feel superior. They seemed so dumb and even dumber in not realizing their dumbness. They gave all of us truth and they gave all of us innocence, always in a laugh. They are still plying us with truth and innocence and laughter in a time when those three wonders are less and less prevalent.

CHAPTER **2**

The Man Behind the Woman
(Burns and Allen)

The room's not too bright. Dad's in the easy chair reading the paper for the third time and Mom's in the dining room fitting out a new pattern for a print dress. You're playing marbles and trying to look casual since it's near your bedtime. Dad jumps up and you figure it's curtains.

"It's late, it's late, turn it on, quick!"

Mom rushes over and flicks on the switch and you are saved for a while, at least until a commercial and they have time to remember you're up too late. You stay immobile and very quiet as they huddle around the five-foot-high wooden box. Sometimes you close your eyes to watch.

MAN: It's one o'clock in the morning. Put away those silly movie magazines and let's get some sleep!

WOMAN: Did you know that Charles Boyer was awful bashful as a boy?

MAN: Oh, turn out the light.

WOMAN: It says here he didn't get his first kiss until he was nine and even then he wasn't thrilled.

MAN: No, huh?

WOMAN: No. I guess those French generals aren't very attractive.

MAN: Turn out the light.

WOMAN: The article I'm reading now is fascinating. "Charles Boyer's Ten Rules for Being a Successful Lover."

MAN: *Turn out the light!*
WOMAN: That's the first rule!

The time is the early '30s, the wooden box is a radio, the man is George Burns and the woman is Gracie Allen.

Few other comedy teams can match the longevity *and* the popularity of Burns and Allen. Until Gracie's retirement in 1958 they had been a constantly working, constantly popular team for thirty-six years, and in the "big time" since the late '20s. Part of the reason for their durability was that their act did not vary from a sound formula, whether in vaudeville, on the radio, in film shorts or features, or on television; when you watched George and Gracie you knew what you were getting. Another secret to their success was that they added new dimensions to their formula in various ways. Their dialogue remained pretty much the same—George being the logical straight man and Gracie being the lovable wacko who's illogical logic seemed more logical than George's logical logic. But Gracie was always fresh and new, whether it was a new routine or not, and the various media changes helped them enormously.

A vaudeville audience was, by definition, small. Burns and Allen expanded with radio and, concurrently, began being seen in movie theaters. The change to television was the capper, making them as close as neighbors, the wise choice being to picture them in their own surroundings. But they weren't always together and they weren't always a team.

Nathan Birnbaum was George's given name. He was born in New York City in 1896 into a big family of seven sisters and five brothers. His father died early. George had to leave school (much to his approval) at thirteen to help support the family. He had shown his interest in show business at age seven by organizing the Pee Wee Quartet. It was his first money-making endeavor; the quartet passed hats in local taverns and on street corners and did not have to pay an agent.

Grace Ethel Cecile Rosalie Allen was Gracie's given name and she was born in San Francisco in 1906, after George had begun his producing ventures. Gracie's father was a song-and-dance man. She debuted in her father's act at three and a half, replete with top hat and "red sluggers" (whiskers). Gracie had three older sisters and a brother and was educated in a parochial school. She also left school at fourteen to join her sisters in a vaudeville act, which led them to the Larry Reilly Company. Gracie was featured in the act and stayed with it after her sisters left—until she argued with Mr. Reilly about still being called "Company." She specialized in Irish ingenue roles, the ingenuous character of the roles never leaving her onstage character although the Irish brogue did leave after much effort.

After the Pee Wees got too big to be called pee wees, George matriculated to vaudeville, appearing in various acts. He tried almost anything to make it in the big time. That was the vaudeville term for the measure of your importance (and endurance) and has come down to us as a catch-all phrase for just being successful. The small time in vaudeville meant that you had to do three or four shows a day and sometimes five on Saturday and/or Sunday. In the big time you only did two shows a day. There were other distinctions in vaudeville: the location and size of your dressing room, your place on the bill (before the seals or after the seals could become particularly important if you were in a dance act).

Georgie, as Gracie called him later, roller-skated, danced, sang, worked with dogs, and changed his name almost weekly to make sure that no one would recognize it and not hire him as a result of remembering his work. Hence, he was Williams one week, Glide the next, and Company of Fry and

Company the following week. He finally wound up with Billy Lorraine doing a song-and-dance act. They received some moderate success but decided to split up. They were playing their last date at the Union Hill Theater in New Jersey when Gracie happened to catch their show.

Gracie had never made the big time with Reilly and, after leaving his show and finding the going rough, had left the business for a secretarial career. She was warned against George Burns by a friend (according to George) and so was introduced to George (by George himself) as his partner, Billy Lorraine. He liked her and thought they might make a team, so he asked her to do an act and she agreed. A week later he told her that he was George Burns and not Billy Lorraine.

Burns and Allen became a team in 1922, but at first it was more Allen and Burns, Gracie being the "straight man" (since she was female, "talking woman" would have been proper) and George giving the payoff or laugh lines. A straight man was the person whom the comedian played against; he or she set up the jokes and the comic would give the punch line for the payoff (laugh).

GEORGE (*as straight man*): A funny thing happened to my mother in Cleveland.
GRACIE (*as comedian*): I thought you were born in Buffalo.
GEORGE: Music!

After their first show in Newark, New Jersey, George quickly found out that the act wasn't working with him giving the punch lines. The audience was laughing at the straight lines that the petite Gracie delivered. One reviewer went so far as to state that Gracie could probably go a long way "if she worked alone." So George took his ego in hand and wisely reversed the act; he played straight and Gracie was the comedienne (or comic person). After the change they started gaining momentum and never slowed down, an unusual claim for a comedy team.

Their first routine, which George wrote, was called "Dizzy" and they played the "small big time" on the Loew's circuit. As their success grew, so did George's affection for the young woman he described as a "living Irish doll." Gracie was in love with someone else but George finally won out, after dropping most of his salary on flowers and other gifts. They were married in January 1926, becoming an official team the same year that Stan Laurel teamed up with Oliver Hardy.

They started a new act around this time and signed a long-term contract with the Keith theater chain that sent them touring the U.S. and Europe. The new routine, written by a veteran comedy gag man, was called "Lamb Chops" and became established as their most famous piece of business.

GEORGE: Do you like love?
GRACIE: No.
GEORGE: Do you like to kiss?
GRACIE: No.
GEORGE: What do you like?
GRACIE: Lamb chops.

The original material in "Lamb Chops" was worked over and honed to a sure laugh-getter. It led Georgie and Googie (as George called Gracie) from the Orpheum to the peak of vaudeville, the Palace Theater in New York. By that time they were headliners and in 1930 played a bill at the Palace with Eddie Cantor and George Jessel that informally marked the end of vaudeville.

In 1929, before they were to tour England, the Warner Brothers asked them to do a film short at their New York studio and George found it impossible to turn down $1,700 for nine minutes' work. The job came along accidentally; they replaced Fred Allen, who was ill. At the same time Paramount started a series of one- and two-reelers with vaudeville stars and signed George and Gracie to do four a year, which turned out to be Warner's loss. Most of the ten-minute shorts were similar to the routines and variations in their stage act and, like their first one for Paramount, *I Want to Buy a Tie*, George did the writing.

After filming their nine-minute epic for Paramount they continued on to England and made their radio debut on the BBC. When they returned to do the Palace bill with Cantor, he asked Gracie to guest on his radio program. She agreed to work without George if Cantor would use one of their routines. Cantor agreed and the show went well. As a result George and Gracie were asked to guest on various shows and soon became regulars on "The Guy Lombardo Show." CBS offered them a contract for their own radio program and they did their first show in early 1932.

In that same year they made their first feature film, again for Paramount. *The Big Broadcast* [of 1932] starred Bing Crosby and Stuart Erwin. Burns and Allen made fourteen shorts from 1929 to 1954 and fourteen features together (Gracie made three features by herself, the last in 1944). But they were never as successful in film as they were in vaudeville, radio, and TV for many of the reasons that Laurel and Hardy and, in later movies, the Marx Brothers were uncomfortable in feature length films. The inherent weakness of the extended plots that tried to interweave the differing elements of a comedy team and subplots just did not hold up for ninety or more minutes. Burns and Allen were at an advantage over Laurel and Hardy and the Marx Four because they did not have to have constant young lovers lolling about and putting everyone to sleep. Usually they were cast against other comedians and stars, such as W. C. Fields, Fred Astaire, Charlie Ruggles, Bob Hope, Jack Oakie, and

George Burns and Gracie Allen as they looked in the heydays of their TV series in the 1950s. (*Courtesy George Burns*)

Jack Benny. Probably their best feature is *Damsel in Distress* with Astaire (minus Ginger Rogers).

Their bread and butter was first vaudeville, then radio for twenty years, and then television. Their radio show, a must in the thirties and forties, was based on material that was akin to "Dizzy" and "Lamb Chops."

GEORGE: Did the nurse ever happen to drop you on your head when you were a baby?

GRACIE: Oh, no, we couldn't afford a nurse, my mother had to do it.

GEORGE: You had a smart mother.

GRACIE: Smartness runs in my family. When I went to school I was so smart my teacher was in my class for five years.

GEORGE: Gracie, what school did you go to?

GRACIE: I'm not allowed to tell.

GEORGE: Why not?

GRACIE: The school pays me twenty-five dollars a month not to tell.

The radio show had over 45 million listeners and the team grossed over $9,000 a week. Among the many running gags in the show, two stood out as the comic counterpart of Orson Welles's hoaxing of America with H. G. Wells's *War of the Worlds* played as a real newscast of an invasion from Mars. In 1933 Gracie began searching the country for her long-lost brother. She would pop up on various shows, such as Jack Benny's or a daytime soap opera, and ask about her brother. The hoax finally ended when Gracie appeared on a rival network show that wouldn't go for the CBS shenanigans that upped the rating and when her real brother, George Allen, an accountant in San Francisco, had to go into hiding.

The second stunt took on even larger proportions. Gracie ran for President in 1940 as a candidate of the Surprise Party. Gracie toured the country by train, making whistle-stops and describing her platform ("redwood trimmed with 'nutty' pine"), wrote a magazine article entitled, "Why America's Next President Should Be a Woman," and held a three-day convention in Omaha. Election time came and she garnered a few hundred write-in votes and led the way for the unsuccessful campaign waged by comedian Pat Paulsen in 1972. Later (in 1944) Gracie actually covered the Democratic and Republican conventions for a national paper.

In 1934 George and Gracie moved to Hollywood and adopted their first child, Sandra Jean. The following year they adopted again, this time a son, Ronald John. With age and responsibility becoming apparent, they decided to change the act formally from a girl-boy relationship to a husband-wife team and it remained that way until Gracie retired from the act.

Another reason for the change in professional marital status might have been the forerunner of TV's dreaded rating system. The ratings of the Burns and Allen radio show had slipped, prompting the loss of one sponsor and their being given a reduction in revenue by their new sponsor. By 1950, after the change, their ratings were back up. That year, after an SRO (standing room only) engagement at the Palladium in London the year before, they decided to plunge into the icy waters of the new and unpredictable medium called television. Others were hesitant and, indeed, George had to talk Gracie into it but, after wisely deciding on the move, they started a biweekly show based on the same format as the radio show.

Although advised by his agent to go into TV while it was an unknown entity, it was George Burns's know-how that kept the whole project afloat: he maintained the same elements as in the live act, with Gracie ignoring the audience/camera and George playing to the audience/camera and commenting. George always maintained that you could not talk down to an audience. Gracie's character as the inane wife of the glib George was never allowed to be "cutesy" and the duo only did things that were commensurate with their age and place in life. They also incorporated their announcer, as in radio days, and he (Bill Goodwin) was worked into the plots as the foil for both George and Gracie.

The show was a winner, and after two years they began filming it as a weekly series. The producer was Fred de Cordova (who now produces the Johnny Carson show), Harry Von Zell replaced Goodwin as the announcer, and the Mortons, the next-door neighbors, were played by Bea Benadaret and Fred Clark (who had replaced Hal March). In time Fred left for Broadway and Larry Keating became Harry Morton; Ronnie Burns, George and Gracie's son, joined the show after a few years. The writers—Harvey Helm, Sid Dorfman, Keith Fowles, and Willie Burns (George's brother)—always stayed with the slow and easy style that George required. George's monologues to the audience, usually commenting on Gracie's complicated ploys, were later linked with a TV–within–a–TV device: George had a set in his den that showed him what was going on as Gracie perpetrated her well-meaning but convoluted schemes. The device added to the fun and the anticipation in the same way that Laurel and Hardy's slowing down of the violent physical exchanges built up the audience anticipation. In the instance of George's TV device, it also heightened the irony that the audience experienced.

A two-camera technique was used on the show and in those unsophisticated times the development of camera technique was part of the early series. One camera would frame the shot in what is called a master and another would either follow action that led out of the framing or zero in on whatever character would be doing a take or a bit of important action. Gracie worked best, whether on stage or in a TV studio, with a minimum of stage directions. She put up a fourth wall—the fourth wall being a term that denotes an imaginary wall in front of the audience/camera which most actors use to develop a sense of reality in what they are doing and to facilitate their concentration on their character and that character's actions and reactions.

The freshness of the show was maintained by a lightning-fast schedule. The scripts were approximately forty or more pages and they rehearsed one day and shot the next. The first day the script was rehearsed in sequence so the actors would know what their emotions were from the beginning of the show through the middle to the end. They were also given their blocking (where they were supposed to go and when they were supposed to go there), the moves, entrances, and exits on that first day. The next day they filmed out of sequence from set-up to set-up of the various locations (Burns's home, Interior; Morton's home, Exterior, etc.). George insisted on shooting the show live. As television matured a host of comedy series used sound tracks of people laughing (laugh tracks) instead of live audiences, but all the better shows in the seventies (as Norman Lear's early contributions attest) took the hint from George and shot live.

The show was a hit for eight years, which is a long run on television, and they filmed nearly three hundred segments (a segment is one in a series of shows). They were still at the top of the ratings when Gracie finally retired, after wanting to do so for quite some time. Beside her performing she had written a syndicated column for a newspaper during her radio days and was an artist in the Surrealist manner. In 1938 she had given an exhibition of her work in a Manhattan gallery in support of the China Aid Council. Unlike her auditory and visual image, Gracie was a multifaceted woman whose talent and insight were tested to the hilt by living and working with the ever mordant Georgie. So, on June 4, 1958, the last episode of "The Burns and Allen Show" was filmed and Gracie left show business at the age of fifty-two.

George, who was sixty-two, felt he was just beginning and

refused to make jokes about the old actors' home. After a brief vacation he started a new career. First he tried his own TV show with the same cast minus Gracie, but that turned out to be, in George's words, "like having dinner . . . but the main course was home playing with her grandchildren." He then opted for cabarets and he opened in Harrah's Club in Tahoe as a monologist and singer, his tenor voice of earlier years now a raspy, but pleasant, baritone. He was not as comfortable as he might have been if Gracie had been onstage instead of in the audience. In 1962 George did an act with Carol Channing that was similar to his old vaudeville routines with Gracie.

Gracie died on August 7, 1964. George had trouble adjusting to the loss for quite a while but, after six months, he returned to performing, his next venture being a TV series with Connie Stevens as the goofy Gracie-like partner in "Wendy and Me." But no one could replace Gracie. George confined himself to nightclubs and guest appearances on TV and his production company produced some specials and a long-running series. Finally, Georgie got his big break at seventy-nine. George's closest friend, whom he had known before his marriage to Gracie, was Jack Benny. Jack was to play the role of Al Lewis in Neil Simon's *The Sunshine Boys*, a Broadway play being made into a movie. The plot involved two aging vaudevillians who had been a successful comedy team in the days that George and Gracie had been hits. George was originally supposed to read for the role of the other partner, Willie Clark, but he missed the reading for an "uncomfortable" day of open-heart surgery; Walter Matthau got the role.

When Jack Benny died, his agent asked George about doing the role Jack was supposed to do. George, with some misgivings, agreed to do it and, in 1975, at eighty years of age, he won an Academy Award for best supporting actor. George is still going strong. He published his second book,

**George Burns in the late 70s after receiving an Academy Award
in the 1975 film, *The Sunshine Boys* and, seemingly, preparing to
play God in the film, *Oh God* (1977). (*Courtesy George Burns*)**

and recently starred as God in a Carl Reiner movie (*Oh,
God*). He played another starring role in the film version of
the Beatles' *Sgt. Pepper's Lonely Hearts Club Band* and is
doing specials and guest shots on TV. George has a number
of film roles lined up and, since the death of Bing Crosby,
is slated to team up with Bob Hope in the planned Hope–

Crosby sequel to their *Road* films, *The Road to the Fountain of Youth.*

Burns and Allen were a viable team, never taking the nose dive that Laurel and Hardy and most other teams did, for a number of reasons. George was amazingly good at what he did and, after realizing what he did best and what Gracie did best, he never varied the formula. His is a case of intelligence winning out over selfishness and ego. George has described his job as Gracie's partner as one of the easiest in the world:

GEORGE: How's your brother?
  (Gracie talks for five minutes.)
GEORGE: Is that so?
  (Gracie talks for another five minutes.)
GEORGE: A bicycle without a chain?
  (Gracie goes for another three.)
GEORGE: No!
  (Gracie does an Irish jig, George taps his toe, they exit.)

It wasn't quite that simple. George guarded Gracie's character. The charm of Gracie was never allowed to be saccharine, nor unreal, nor cheap. There was always a sincerity and a reality to what she did that was akin to the honesty maintained by Stan and Ollie. Like Laurel and Hardy, George knew that you had to keep the audience above you, not below you. Even in our modern circumstances, Gracie does not seem like the stereotypical housewife who is dominated by her husband. If she is a bit eccentric that eccentricity is alleviated by a number of elements: she always comes out on top. Even though she played a dense woman, other women could feel superior to her *as a person*, as did men—the same way that both men and women felt superior to Laurel and Hardy. Making the audience feel superior is a prime requisite of comedy. Finally, George was the smart aleck, as Oliver had been the know-it-all, while Gracie remained the innocent, sincere, lovable silly-person. George's theory about jokes was quite different from other acts and he became one of the best, most likely *the* best straight man in comedy as a result. Theory: throw the jokes away, never push for a laugh. If you set up a joke that has to get a laugh when you're done speaking and you stop and there is silence, you are in trouble. Not only with that joke, your whole credibility is in jeopardy. If you are a real person, flesh and blood, an honest person, say a George Burns or a Gracie Allen, and the laugh doesn't come, it doesn't matter. People like you for what you are and how you say things, not for what you say. If you happen to have a few good gags up your sleeve, great, but if not . . . see you next week, same time, same place. It worked.

GEORGE: Which came first, the chicken or the egg?
GRACIE: I didn't even know they were here. I better go to the store.

CHAPTER 3

Three Madmen and Two Guys Who Were a Little Peeved (The Marx Brothers)

MINNIE MARX: Where else can people who don't know anything make a living?

The guy running around in the blond Afro and honking an old car horn instead of talking was Adolph, but Adolph was not blond and could talk. The one who was selling his brother's wife (house, car, or child) and talking in a broken Italian accent was not a salesman, nor was he Italian. His name was Leonard. Lusting after women at the drop of almost anything, the third wore large glasses, had a painted-on mustache, carried a large cigar, and walked hunched over, as if trying to make a smaller target for irate husbands. But Julius did not have a bad back and eventually stopped using his upper lip for an artist's canvas. He did not stop lusting after women. No one really remembers Milton, but he did exist, and Herbert, to present it fairly, was the youngest. Put into the computer, this reads out The Marx Brothers.

The Marx Brothers, like many performers and most comedians, were poor, quit school at a young age to work, and came from a family that had a theatrical background. The boys' grandparents on their mother's side had performed professionally in their native Germany. Lafe Schoenberg had been a magician-ventriloquist and his wife Fanny was a harpist who yodeled. They emigrated to America when their daughter Minnie was fifteen. Apparently American audiences did not take to harpists who yodeled or magicians who talked to themselves, so Lafe took the next logical career move and began repairing umbrellas.

Minnie Schoenberg met her future husband Sam ("Frenchie") Marx at a school where he taught dancing. They were married when she was eighteen. Sam, taking a cue from his father-in-law Lafe, gave up dancing to become a tailor of questionable merit.

Minnie and Sam Marx had five children: Leonard in 1887, Adolph (Arthur) the next year, Julius Henry (1890), Milton in 1897, and finally Herbert in 1901. Although no one has ever heard of these five men, they were later rechristened at a poker game in Rockford, Illinois (so the story goes), and everyone recognized the imposters at once and demanded payment of old debts. Leonard chased "chicks" and was named Chicko. A printing error changed it to Chico. Adolph's harp playing garnered his title Harpo; grouchy, irascible Julius became Groucho; Milton was named Gummo after the current slang for a detective ("gumshoe"). Later Herbert joined the act as Zippo and reacted in a very un-Marx-like way by changing it to Zeppo.

The boys grew up on the upper East Side of New York City, a Jewish family in a predominantly German and Irish environment. They moved frequently because of a lack of money. As a result, the brothers learned to hustle at an early age. Chico, as the eldest, became the most adept at any form of acquiring money. Minnie insisted on a musical background for the boys so Chico was given piano lessons. Somehow they managed the quarter-a-lesson fee. Chico was supposed to pass on his knowledge to Harpo but he had other important matters to attend to and Harpo was drawn to his grandmother's instrument, the harp. Chico played piano in beer gardens as soon as he was able, in an attempt to pay off his constant gambling debts from pool, craps, horses, and cards. It was a lifelong endeavor. He also made a habit of pawning anything in the house that was not attached to the wall or someone's hand.

Harpo did odd jobs: walking dogs, setting pins in a bowling alley, bellhopping, and so on. He was the clown of the group and did imitations of neighborhood characters when he wasn't lost in his fantasy world or playing the harp. Groucho wanted to be a doctor for a while but then changed to writing as his goal, the latter requiring no expensive years in college. To this end he read more than the others and was regarded as the intellectual. Groucho also sang, his soprano voice blending with Chico's piano, the guitar of Gummo and Minnie, Sam's mandolin and, perhaps, the beginning plucks on Harpo's harp, when the family got together for a night of music.

Gummo and Zeppo were eclipsed by their elder brothers. This manifested itself later with Gummo dropping from the act first and, after Zeppo replaced him, the act again reverting to a threesome after their sixth film *Duck Soup*.

CAPTAIN SPAULDING: As I say, I was sitting in front of the cabin when I bagged six tigers. This was the biggest lot . . .
MRS. RITTENHOUSE: Oh, Captain, Captain, did you catch six tigers?
CAPTAIN SPAULDING: I bagged them. I bagged them to go away. But they hung around all afternoon. They were the most persistent tigers I have ever seen.

This exchange between Groucho as the captain and Margaret Dumas as the stuffy, rich dowager in the film *Animal Crackers* is not the way the Marx Brothers started out. First of all, they did not start as a team. Second, given their musical background, the emphasis was on singing. Groucho had toured as a boy singer. He wound up in a singing trio with Gummo and a friend, Lou Levy. Harpo joined the trio when he was fourteen and promptly wet his pants. His fear in front of a live audience led to his developing the mute character that communicated in outlandish pantomime.

Minnie was the boys' mentor in show business and organized their early attempts. The Four Nightingales (Groucho, Gummo, Harpo, and a fourth boy) became the Six Mascots under her guidance. She added herself and her sister Hannah to the act because acts were paid by the number of people in them. Chico had started out as an accompanist on the piano and played blindfolded. He developed the act into a single in clubs. Disliking performing even more than Harpo did, Gummo left for the army in World War I and never returned to show business. Zeppo took his place.

The act consisted of singing with some dancing by chorus girls in the background and some comedy bits. The transition from a singing act with very little comedy to a comedy act with very little singing evolved over the years from their first group efforts in 1908 and 1909 to a more or less final version in the early twenties. Chico abandoned his blindfold and joined the others after they had started the changeover to comedy. Articulating the various steps that brought about the chemistry of the Marx Brothers is impossible. Suffice it to say that ad libs became an integral part of their sketches somewhere along the way and the nonverbal humor of Harpo became bigger and wackier. Like most vaudevillians, they developed routines by trial and error. One of the tested subjects at the time was school, so they came up with "Fun in Hi Skule." Two later pieces, "Mr. Green's Reception" and "Home Again," were written by their uncle, Al Shean. Shean had given them help and encouragement and was a headliner himself in the famous vaudeville team of Gallagher and Shean. The brothers had always felt free to make fun of themselves and their own bits, and this, of course, tied in with the constant ad libs.

During this formative period they toured the country on

the various circuits. The work on the act singled out distinct characters that came across as full portraits in the later films. Harpo, due to his fear, lack of delivery, and a hesitancy to do a repeat of his debut, came up with a character out of silent films and the circus. The battered hobo's hat, the fright wig, the tattered raincoat with the outsized pockets for his many props, and the bulb horn from an antique car, became his identity. Having clowned and mugged as a kid, imitating the neighborhood eccentrics, he now used it as an effective comedy device.

Dialect humor was fashionable during the period, most likely due to the enormous number of immigrants who still had difficulty with English. Chico had picked up dialects readily as a kid in the streets of New York, so his parody of an Italian immigrant's speech was logical and accepted in good taste. Groucho, like many comedians before and after (George Burns, Milton Berle, and Alan King come to mind), found that a cigar was a useful prop. He also did a German accent for a while but later dropped it for his typical New Yorkese. If a bushy mustache had worked for other comedians, why not paint a mustache over your lip? He did. Zeppo, playing the straight man, never developed any comedy type and comes off bland next to the others. He lacked the timing and the ingenuity of the true straight man like George Burns.

The brothers almost didn't make the Palace in 1915 but finally did after Minnie harried the management from reneging on the booking. The boys got the worst spot on the vaudeville bill, opening the show. To manager Albee's chagrin, they did so well that they were jumped to the best spot, next to closing. More troubles with the manager, who owned most of the better vaudeville houses, got them blacklisted. They found themselves with diminished pay and fewer bookings but they had one ace in the hole. Chico managed to hustle a fellow poker player into backing a show that led them to Broadway in 1924.

The show was *I'll Say She Is*. They toured it for over a year and then opened at the Casino Theater to rave reviews. The most respected and the most difficult critic at the time was Alexander Woollcott. His review of the musical made them a hit. They then had three straight successes, the next two being *The Cocoanuts* in 1925 and *Animal Crackers* in 1928.

Even though Groucho lost a great deal in the stock market crash of 1929, the same year that many silent screen stars were ruined by talking pictures, the Marx Brothers were not unfavorably affected. Before they reached the Palace, long before they hit Broadway, they were making $1,500 a week. Paramount Studios augmented the shorts they had been filming with vaudeville headliners with full-length talkies and they signed the four brothers to a three-film contract for a little under a quarter of a million dollars.

While *Animal Crackers* was still running on Broadway, Groucho, Chico, Harpo, and Zeppo filmed their previous stage hit *The Cocoanuts* at Paramount's Astoria studios on Long Island. Although they had dabbled in an early silent film entitled *Humorisk*, no one was happier than they were when the original copy of the fiasco was lost. Harpo had done a solo in *Too Many Kisses* with William Powell in 1925, but he was, to his dismay, almost completely cut out of the film. For the most part, the Marx Four were uninitiated in camera techniques; fortunately, they didn't need to be. Even given the static quality or staginess of the film, the brothers cavort with the same crazy razzle-dazzle that comes through for them over and over again. The picture was an enormous triumph.

The one sad twist was the death of Minnie Marx in September 1929. She was allotted the time to see their first film and their establishment as cinema stars as well as Broadway heavyweights. Many years later she was depicted in the

Left to right, Chico, Groucho, Harpo, and Zeppo Marx during
the filming of their second film *Animal Crackers* in 1930. They
frequently participated in Conga lines on saw horses. (*Wide
World Photos*)

early 1970s Broadway musical *Minnie's Boys*, which starred
Shelley Winters as Momma Marx.

After the New York run they toured *Animal Crackers* and
it was the obvious choice for their second film. As Laurel and
Hardy had taken the gags for their upcoming films on tour to
try them out, the Marx Brothers had the added advantage of
playing the material for their first two films before hundreds
of audiences. They had a pretty good idea of what was
funny and what was not. The same procedure had worked
with their vaudeville routines and they saw no point in
changing—for a while.

Later there were critical comments but these were leveled
at elements that were intrusions by others or at material that
was untested. The closing shots of *The Cocoanuts* and the

later *A Day at the Races* have been singled out and they are, indeed, foreign to the Marx Brothers' style. The former closes with the brothers waving to the camera and then zeroing in on the ever-present, ever-singing, ever-boring young lovers, and the latter ends with the cast marching along the racetrack toward the camera while revamping the score. But there are more durable criticisms, the last few frames of a movie certainly not being the sum of the parts. Until their first hiatus from filming, the Marx Brothers were always consistently funny. If some films do not hang together, the fault lies in the writing, directing, and producing.

Monkey Business, their third film, was an original script written expressly for them and for the screen. It was not as solid but was well received and, if lacking the flair of the first two, it was good fun. The year 1932 brought out *Horse Feathers,* another original, and it kept them on an even keel with the critics. They almost left Paramount before *Duck Soup,* but returned after a brief flirtation with theatrical producer Sam Harris, who was originally partnered with George M. Cohan. This film was different from anything they had tried before in that it was a pointed political satire. As Laurel and Hardy and others had found before, reviewers and the public are not comfortable with political satire and the film was not as productive as previous efforts. Zeppo decided finally to leave the act after this venture and became an agent.

The lackluster showing of *Soup* led the three remaining comics to the renowned producer Irving Thalberg, at MGM. Under his auspices they found their greatest acclaim in the 1935 *A Night at the Opera.* Thalberg instituted the young lovers' convention in a balanced way, and with Groucho, Chico, and Harpo allowed to be lunatics once more, it worked well for all concerned. They toured the material before filming, as in earlier days, and the enormous response to the film brought about what is now called a sequel: *A Day at the*

Races. This film was not nearly as good and was received accordingly. Many, including Groucho, felt that the step down was due to the death of Thalberg three weeks into the shooting schedule. As a result, there was an untempered indulgence in the inane romantic-musical interludes and the previously mentioned mishmash rehash of tunes that closes the movie indicating the lack of consistency to the Marx style. (There is no way to prove that Groucho's assessment of Thalberg's influence is correct; despite his many innovative ideas, Thalberg fought the intrusion of music as background for film when it was suggested. Today it is impossible to conceive of film without background music for emphasis and completeness.)

The reviewers disapproved of the film but the public paid more money to see it than they had for the critical hit of *A Night at the Opera.* As Groucho might say, so much for the critics. There is no faulting the Marx Brothers' work in either film. *Races* was just not the synthesis that *Opera* had been, a synthesis that is necessary to make a film a whole.

Concurrent with the later film work, the three zanies had been doing a radio show called "Flywheel, Shyster, and Flywheel," the name reminiscent of various law firms mentioned in their movies. The show was all right but radio was not their most effective medium as a team. It did work out for Groucho later but his humor was more verbally oriented than Chico's. The disappointment of *A Day at the Races* started a downward spiral in the effectiveness of their films. In 1938 they returned to MGM to try something slightly different. This time they were going to take a proven Broadway play, producer-director George Abbott's *Room Service,* and adapt it to their format and the cinema medium. The transference did not pan out and, although amusing, *Room Service* strains on and on without enough of the old flavor.

Next they made a number of movies that were inferior to even the lesser preceding ones: *At the Circus, Go West,* and

The Big Store. After this trio of downbeat experiences, the
three brothers who now made up the team left films in
1941 for five years and followed varied solo pursuits. Harpo
did USO tours and made a promotional short for 20th Century-Fox; Chico formed a band and played all over the country, occasionally doing radio shows; Groucho made guest
appearances on numerous radio shows. Gummo and Zeppo
quietly pursued their careers as agents out of the public eye.

A Night in Casablanca, made for United Artists in 1946,
attempted to cash in on the *Opera* and *Races* movies as
well as the recent hit made by Humphrey Bogart and
Ingrid Bergman in *Casablanca.* It was a welcomed return of
the Italian, the Mustache, and the Honker but it was not
thoroughly triumphant. The brothers even invested in the
film but did not earn a profit. Three years later they made an
independently produced film, *Love Happy,* but it minimized
the on-screen presence of their usual antics with Groucho
making almost a token appearance as the narrator. This experience led to another "retirement" but, as a team, this was
the final appearance of the Marx Brothers except for a half-
hour segment for the "G.E. Theater" series on television in
1959. This venture, "The Incredible Jewel Robbery," was
definitely not vintage Marx Brothers' fare. Since 1959, except
for reruns on late night TV or in enlightened movie theaters,
people no longer heard exchanges like the following from
Go West:

QUALE [Groucho]: Panello, this Indian is no Indian!
PANELLO [Chico]: If he's 'a no Indian, why is he wearin' a
  chicken for a hat?

But they might hear Groucho echo *Animal Crackers:*

CAPTAIN SPAULDING: The principal animals inhabiting the African
  jungle are Moose, Elks and Knights of Pythias.

Or:

> You ought to brush up on your Greek, Jamison. Well, get a
> Greek and brush up on him.

Groucho was the only one of the brothers to expand and
remain a popular figure after the demise of the team. He
started a radio show called "You Bet Your Life" in 1947 and,
following the lead of other teams (Burns and Allen, Abbott
and Costello), made a healthy transition to television in the
fifties. "You Bet Your Life" utilized a quiz-show format but
there was a minimum of tension and hoopla and a maxi-
mum of Groucho's quips and ad libs. Overall the show ran
for almost ten years. A second effort on TV, "Tell It to
Groucho," only lasted a season but the original quiz show
was syndicated as "The Best of Groucho" in the mid-1970s
and can still be seen in some parts of the country. Late-
night television has brought back testy and teasing Groucho
to older fans and a whole new generation of devotees. Near
the end of his life, Groucho was asked if he was surprised at
the tremendous reception of the reruns of "You Bet Your
Life." He responded characteristically, "Of course not, it's on
opposite the news."

Julius Henry also got to fulfill his boyhood wish and write
—for pay! He co-scripted a play (*Time for Elizabeth*) and a
film (*The King and the Chorus Girl*) with Norman Krasna
and he wrote five books, including his autobiography,
Groucho and Me. His last book, *The Secret World of
Groucho*, appeared in 1975.

Groucho, in his eighties, still made appearances on rare
occasions in the early 1970s. If his wit was not as quick as
it formerly was, it was still sufficient to deal with most talk-
show hosts. In 1949 Groucho starred without his brothers in
Copacabana and he made subsequent solo appearances in
Mr. Music (1950), *Double Dynamite* (with Frank Sinatra,
1951), *A Girl in Every Port* (1952), *Will Success Spoil Rock*

Hunter? (1957), and, for Otto Preminger, *Skidoo* in 1968. Groucho had been in retirement for years but he returned in 1972 to do a triumphant one-man show all over the country and sold out Carnegie Hall. He also guested on the Dick Cavett and Johnny Carson talk shows. The same year he was honored by the French government with a special award at the Cannes Film Festival commemorating the contribution of the Marx Brothers to world cinema. In failing health, Groucho died in August 1977 at the age of eighty-six. But as long as there is film, he will live.

After *Love Happy*, Chico, or Ravelli, as astute fans remember him, worked only sporadically. He did a club act with Harpo in Las Vegas during the fifties and a lead in the road show of the Broadway comedy, *The Fifth Season*. In 1957 Irwin Allen, now known for his disaster films, made a disastrous film entitled *The Story of Mankind*, in which Harpo was Sir Isaac Newton and Groucho and Chico did cameo roles that are better left unmentioned. Chico did a "Playhouse 90" and a commercial short with Groucho in 1958 ("Showdown at Ulcer Gulch") but, ever the hustler, Chico was beleaguered by debts and ill health, and died in 1961 at seventy-four.

In addition to the club act with Chico and his portrayal of Sir Isaac, in 1952 Harpo almost played the lead role in RKO's film of George Bernard Shaw's *Androcles and the Lion*. What would have been extremely innovative casting was vetoed by the head of the studio, Howard Hughes, who denied Harpo the part. The mime artist guested on assorted TV shows, including Lucille Ball's situation comedy "I Love Lucy." Unlike Marcel Marceau, Harpo never spoke on film. Like Chico, he was a victim of heart trouble and died at seventy-five in 1964. Gummo had become a clothes manufacturer in New York after he left show business and in 1933 he moved to Hollywood to represent his brothers. He continued as their agent and joined Zeppo when his younger brother formed the Zeppo Marx Agency in 1935. When the agency was taken over by one of the larger conglomerates, Gummo continued to manage Groucho's affairs through the early sixties. Gummo died of natural causes in 1977. Zeppo pursued various nontheatrical interests and now lives in retirement in Palm Springs.

The Marx Brothers' career spanned more than forty years as a team, which is a long stretch for duos, even longer for trios and quartets. If Groucho is singled out, as he must be, his longevity extends to sixty years, or more than eighty years if his early start as a performer is considered. The reason for this long-term appreciation by audiences is manifold. If Laurel and Hardy relied primarily on visual humor as their mainstay, even after the switch to talkies, and Burns and Allen emphasized the verbal throughout their radio and television days, the Marx Brothers were a combination of the two forms of communication in comedy.

They did sight gags, and Harpo, Chico, and Groucho had superb timing—the element that makes comedy work, and without which a good joke is bad and a bad joke is worse. Groucho's crouched, stalking walk, his overstated eyebrows wiggling up and down over his rolling eyes, the constantly flicked cigar, and the oversized mustache (whether painted on or, as in later years, real) created an indelible image. To this day audiences recognize the most rotten Groucho impression. It does not matter who does it, if it's live, if it's on one of the media, they recognize it. And yet he was the most word-oriented comic of the three. Harpo is idolized by some because of the pathos and simplicity of his mute clown character. In terms of action, he was the most fantastically big of the three. Chico, as Panello, was the middle man, talking for Harpo, engaging in physical humor with whomever was near, baiting Groucho, and hustling everyone, including his ward Harpo and, on occasion, himself.

The impact of the Marx Brothers' comedy on the world,

not just the world of television or films, was such that they are the most known and best-loved performers in the world, with the possible exception of Charlie Chaplin. The only team that can match them for universality is Laurel and Hardy, and Stan and Ollie did not engage in the depths of satire that Groucho used to destroy the conventions of almost any society. The brothers went beyond the simple souls portrayed by Laurel and Hardy and beyond the deft timing and turned-upside-down reality of Gracie Allen. They made fun of everything and anything, particularly those things that most of us hold in reverence. They were the kings of irreverence. No one had to worry about whether what they did was within the boundaries of good taste or not, it merely was funny.

As a result of this no-holds-barred attack, they affected the world around them, the humor, the society, the art. Critics, analysts and members of the absurdist school of playwrighting in the late fifties and early sixties have categorically claimed that the films of the Marx Brothers were a direct influence. There are other parallels in art and the list of gaga fans is astoundingly broad, from critic Woollcott to novelist, screenwriter, critic James Agee, from Woody Allen to Dick Cavett, from French playwright Eugene Ionesco to English author Tom Stoppard.

The years of work in vaudeville, refining and improving, polishing and defining, brought almost flawless control and choice to their best films. They have not been matched before, or since. Why? The answer is in a short exchange between Groucho (Hammer) and Chico in the first film *The Cocoanuts.*

HAMMER: Now here's the main road leading out of Cocoanut Manor. That's the road I wish you were on. Now over here— on this site we're going to build an Eye and Ear Hospital. This is going to be a sight for sore eyes. . . . Now here is a little peninsula, and here is a viaduct leading over to the mainland.

CHICO: Why a duck?

HAMMER: I'm all right. How are you? I say here is a little peninsula, and here is a viaduct leading over to the mainland.

CHICO: All right. Why a duck? Why 'a . . . why a duck? Why-a-
no-chicken?

HAMMER: I'm all right. How are you? I say here is a little
myself. All I know is that it's a viaduct. You try to cross over
there a chicken and you'll find out why a duck. It's deep
water, that's viaduct.

CHICO: That's why-a-duck?

HAMMER: . . . All I know is that it's a viaduct.

CHICO: Now look—all righta—I catcha on to why-a-horse, why-a-
chicken, why-a-this, why-a-that. I no catch on to why-a-duck.

HAMMER: . . . I was only fooling. They're going to build a tunnel
in the morning. Now, is that clear to you?

CHICO: Yes. Everything—excepta why-a-duck.

CHAPTER **4**

Who's on Second? (Abbott and Costello)

BUD ABBOTT: Ours is a talking act.
LOU COSTELLO: A loud talking act. One might call it corn.

One of the reasons that we can still laugh easily at some silent films is that they are funny. Their humor stands up. Another reason is that we immediately accept the absence of sound. Once we no longer think it odd that the characters do not actually speak, we also place the whole in a time perspective and accept things that would not make sense in our own time. If the plots are silly, almost nonexistent, and the jokes simplistic, even childish, it is because they are of another time.

Abbott and Costello were never received very well by the critics because they used dated material. Their public, which was large and varied, lasted for a relatively short period of time. The main reason for their not lasting like George and Gracie or the Marx Brothers was this same reliance on humor from vaudeville and burlesque, from a different time. Their style was set and they did not vary it to accommodate changes in society, nor did they give it any depth so that it would grow with them. They have been praised, and rightly so, for preserving many of the old vaudeville and "burlie" routines on film. But because they did not adapt, they did not survive. Their films, which constantly replay on early morning weekend shows, appeal to children. Some of their routines are classic. But too many of their bits are clichéd, hackneyed, and repetitive. With Abbott and Costello we don't accept the convention, we demand that they be funny. And they quite often are not, unless they rely on a piece of material that is ageless.

The premise of "Who's on First" is simply that the first baseman of a baseball team is named Who, the second baseman is named What, and the third baseman is I Don't Know. Without this knowledge, explained in this way, you might find yourself in this situation.

ABBOTT: I say Who's on first, What's on second, I Don't Know's on third.

COSTELLO: Yeah, you know the fellow's name?

ABBOTT: Yes.

COSTELLO: Well, who's on first?

ABBOTT: Yes.

COSTELLO: I mean the fellow's name.

ABBOTT: Yes.

COSTELLO: I mean the guy playing first.

ABBOTT: Who.

COSTELLO: The fellow playing first.

ABBOTT: Who.

COSTELLO: The first baseman.

ABBOTT: Who.

COSTELLO: The guy playing first base.

ABBOTT: Who is on first!

COSTELLO: What are you asking me for?

They progress to second base, third, and finally the shortstop, whose name is I Don't Give a Damn.

About the only similarity between Louis Francis Cristillo (Lou Costello) and William ("Bud") Abbott was that they were both born in the wilds of New Jersey, Bud in Asbury Park in 1895 and Lou in Paterson in 1906. Lou's father was an Italian immigrant, who worked as a weaver and later for an insurance company, and his mother was of Irish descent. Bud's father was an advance man for a circus and his mother was a bareback rider.

Lou's film image as the short (5′4″), rotund dummy was further from the fact than Bud's image as the tall, slim, fast-talking con man. Bud left school after the fourth grade to work around the amusement park at Coney Island. He "shilled," working for the house as a decoy to get others to play at games of chance, and generally accrued material for his slightly dishonest stage and film character. Lou, strangely enough, pursued athletics in school and won a state title in basketball (foul shooting) and was an amateur boxer under the pseudonym Lou King. He had always been a movie fan and in 1927, at twenty-one he hitchhiked to Hollywood with a friend. Finding work was rough but, after months of sleeping in cars and scrounging for food, they hustled some jobs as carpenters and extras. Lou's athletics and short stature got him work as a stunt man, usually doubling for female stars like Dolores Del Rio and Joan Crawford.

Before Lou was old enough to get thrown around on a sound stage, Bud graduated from Coney Island, with an assist from his father, to assistant treasurer at the Casino burlesque theater in Brooklyn. Later he had a short sabbatical, allegedly being shanghaied from a waterfront bar and spending a number of months on a steamer bound for Norway. Returning to box office work, he decided to produce shows with his brother Harry; both the Shubert and the Albee theater chains were in great trouble. When this venture did not pan out, Bud produced shows at the National Theater in Detroit for three years.

Around this time, after a year and a half of grubbing in Hollywood, Lou and his buddy Gene headed back East. When Gene dropped off with relatives in Kansas, Lou wound up at the Lyceum Theater in St. Joseph, Missouri. The theater was looking for a Dutch comic. A "Dutch comic" was merely another variation of the dialect comedy that the Marx Brothers embraced and which had been a staple of American comedy since the nineteenth century. Whatever the requirements, Lou, hot from his long-shot portrayal of Ms. Crawford, got the job. Lou got his initiation as a comedian, which must have been a bit touch-and-go for a few minutes considering that he had only observed before, and gives us all an idea of what passed for humor in Missouri. He adopted the same name as his brother Pat (a saxophonist with his own band) Costello. Lou then returned to Paterson and, in 1930, got his first job as a burlesque comic at the Orpheum Theater in New York.

There he did skits and learned his craft. One of his early routines, "The Schoolroom," was in the mold of the school sketches of the time (the Marx Brothers' first sketch was "Fun in Hi Skule"). Lou was learning to be batted around, physical humor being a large part of both vaudeville and, even more so, burlesque. While Lou was working his way up to top banana, Bud was sharing the limelight with various comics.

He had managed to watch the greats as well as the awfuls during his years in box office and as a producer. Stars like W. C. Fields and Fanny Brice played these houses and Bud learned from all of them. The show-business story has Bud, with no previous experience, filling in for Lou's absent partner one night. The boys publicized this story along with a number of other falsehoods. They both enjoyed duping people and playing practical jokes. It is not surprising, as a result, to find biographies listing Bud as being born in Asbury Park, Coney Island, or Atlantic City at various dates between 1895 and 1898. He was also supposed to have been a lion tamer and an auto racer, although he allegedly never drove a lion or a car. When their career was at its peak, their antics, especially Lou's, got them into trouble. They became difficult to work with and, when their popularity waned, there were not many good feelings to fall back on.

What really happened was that Bud decided to come from the front of the house and perform onstage. His growing years had given him a pat hand: the fast-talking con man. He was a success immediately and comics demanded his talents as their straight man. He developed a physical style that he later incorporated with Lou, pushing, dragging, and knocking down comedians as he fed them their set-ups. The slapping seemed to ingratiate the comic with the audience. The comics liked it. The audience liked it.

Bud's lucrative position as straight man, who usually got 60 percent to the comic's 40 percent, was working out well but he wanted something else. In 1936, teamed with Harry Evanson, he played the Eltinge Theater on West Forty-second Street in New York the same week as a burlesque comic named Lou Costello. They eyed each other approvingly, and over bagels at Reuben's restaurant, they dropped their present partners and became a team. They continued in burlie for the remaining months the genre had left.

Like vaudeville before it, burlesque slowed down, then stopped. In 1937 burlesque shut down in New York City because of its risqué nature. Even though Abbott and Costello were not known to indulge in off-color jokes, burlesque was known for smutty humor and scantily clad women. Mayor La Guardia closed all the burlie houses in the city of New York. The talkies had already brought burlesque to a near-standstill and had shuttered most of the vaudeville houses. The "six-a-days" were gone and the "two-a-days" were going. Abbott and Costello were making it big when it all came to a halt; luckily, they had somewhere to go.

They started their act with "Life Begins at Minsky's," which they toured. Tried and true bits like "Crazy House" and "Who's on First" became known to audiences as Bud and Lou worked their twists on the routines and polished them to a remarkable precision. Their popularity grew due to their diversity; they seemed to pigeonhole and adapt many of the major burlesque routines. They moved to their first nightclub gig in New York and then on to one of the remaining vaudeville houses, Loew's State in New York.

At that time a young comedian wanted to go to Hollywood but couldn't leave his radio job unless he found a replacement. He caught Abbott and Costello at Loew's State and got them the job. In 1938 Bud and Lou did their first "Kate Smith Show" and Henny Youngman went off to seek glory in Tinsel Town. This appearance led to Bud and Lou becoming regulars on the show. They remained in radio until the early fifties. In 1940 they became Fred Allen's summer replacement and had their own show in 1941.

Radio finalized the recognizable elements of their act. Their own show started with Lou's howling, "HEY, AB-BOTT!" And Lou's tag line, "I'm a bad boy," became known all over the country. It also established Lou's squeaky, high-pitched voice. They found on Kate Smith's show that listeners were having trouble differentiating between Bud and Lou's voices. They couldn't tell who was questioning and who was answering. Lou assumed a quasi-falsetto which dovetailed neatly with his developing image as the put-upon, knocked-around, dopey little boy.

The radio exposure led to Broadway and eventually to Hollywood and films. In 1939 they did *The Streets of Paris* in their only appearance on Broadway (at the Broadhurst) and at the New York World's Fair. The show was a revue and easily accommodated the boys' routines and style. They were lucky that they weren't burnt-out, for at one point that year they were doing Kate's radio show, the revue on Broadway, and a nightclub act at the Versailles Club.

In 1940 Universal added them to a musical film entitled *One Night in the Tropics*. The picture was a turkey but Bud and Lou were singled out as the best thing in it. Universal signed them and moved them from supporting roles to starring ones in *Buck Privates*, initiating almost forty films that the duo made together, most of them for Universal.

In 1941 *Buck Privates* was released and became such a hit that three more films were released the same year: *In the Navy, Hold That Ghost,* and *Keep 'Em Flying.* Their success also landed them a contract with another studio, MGM, and after *Ride 'Em Cowboy* at their home studio they did *Rio Rita* for Metro in 1942.

Buck Privates brought them the highest critical acclaim they ever received, with Lou likened to Chaplin and even being touted by the Little Tramp himself as the current "best" in the business. It was a critical time for them to make their film debut. Laurel and Hardy were slumping through their later extended feature films; the Marx Brothers were on their first long hiatus from moviemaking; and George and Gracie were never the standouts in films that they were on radio and TV. Abbott and Costello had a physical, visual comedy that George and Gracie lacked. They were the logical heirs to the number one position.

They made eight more films over the next four years and, except for their first for MGM, *Rio Rita*, they all conformed to the pattern and satisfied their public. *Abbott and Costello in Hollywood,* another MGM loser, got them dropped by that studio in 1945. The previous year, for the first time since *Buck Privates*, they did not make the top ten list of film money-makers.

Bud and Lou had always relied on their routines from vaudeville and burlesque being strung together by a plot that allowed niches for their bits and ad libs. So, "Who's on First," "Crazy House" (with Lou seeing dream people come to life), and "Jonah and the Whale" (used in *Tropics* with Bud not allowing Lou to tell a funny story and then giving the punch line), recur in various forms in their films. Showing the trend of their downward slump in the mid-1940s, *Little Giant* (1946) seems extremely derivative. William A. Seiter, who directed Laurel and Hardy in *Sons of the Desert*, was their director; Margaret Dumont, who played in most of the Marx Brothers' films, appears in her standard stuffy dowager character. The two utilized an old bit from a Laurel and Hardy film (*Berth Marks*), though not even original with L & H, undressing with great difficulty in a tiny train berth. Things were not going well.

The Time of Their Lives, also made in 1946, had the benefit of good writing, directing, and special effects. The duo attempted to give some depth to their static characters of the bad little boy and his con-man substitute father. They succeeded, but not many took notice, so they returned to formula efforts and in 1947 made *Buck Privates Come Home*, a sequel to their first big hit. They made two more films before hitting on an addition to the failing formula that brought them some short-lived popularity.

In their fourth film, *Hold That Ghost*, they had been thrust into a situation that capitalized on horror, the supernatural, and Lou's fear and screaming. In 1948 they made *Abbott and Costello Meet Frankenstein*, initiating a series that had them terrorized by Boris Karloff, the Invisible Man, Captain Kidd, Dr. Jekyll and Mr. Hyde and, finally, the Mummy. Unluckily they also met Jack and the Beanstalk and various other sorts during this final period of their filmmaking. The Frankenstein movie revived public interest in the two for a while but then it dwindled.

Abbott and Costello had matriculated from radio to television in 1951 via "The Colgate Comedy Hour," an hour-long variety show that competed with Ed Sullivan and was hosted on a rotating business by Eddie Cantor, Donald O'Conner, Abbott and Costello, and the rapidly emerging Martin and Lewis. As always, Bud and Lou were criticized for doing old-hat, cornball routines over and over again. And

Bobby Barber (c.), a stooge for Bud Abbott (l.) and Lou Costello (r.), is not pleased that they asked him out for dinner (1951). (*Wide World Photos*)

without the guise of a film plot line, they reverted to chewing up their many routines pretty quickly. In 1953, after Jimmy Durante and Bob Hope had been added to the list of hosts, Abbott and Costello were on the way out. Lou had been ill, and this is usually given as the reason for their not appearing in the '54 season.

The same year as the Colgate show started filming, they began their own series, "The Abbott and Costello Show" for CBS. It ran for only two seasons (fifty-two segments). It began airing in 1952 and made use of thin plot lines to disguise their routines, hoping to create an atmosphere similar to their successful films and prevent the problems they had encountered on the variety series. At the time they were still the highest-paid performers in the business (Martin and

Lewis would soon usurp this position), but that in itself did nothing to prevent the show from receiving bad reviews. Sid Fields played their landlord and various other roles as well as writing many of the shows. Joe Besser, later one of the Three Stooges and in the seventies working consistently doing voice-over work and dubbing as characters on children's cartoon shows, played Stinky. Gordon Jones, from their films, played Mike the cop, and Hillary Brooke, for the first season, was their sympathetic, blond neighbor. Lou's brother-in-law Joe Kirk played Mr. Bacciagalupe and wrote for the show.

The show utilized various bits and one show managed to incorporate "The Baker Scene" (which is earlier but similar to "Who's on First"), "Floogle Street," an old standby, and "Get Out of the Office," which sounds vaguely reminiscent of Smith and Dale's old doctor sketch ("Dr. Kronkhite") that is embellished and twisted by Neil Simon in *The Sunshine Boys*. With the condemnation of the first twenty-six episodes, they attempted to change the second season by toning down the shrill pitch of the first year, dropping three regular characters, hiring a new writer, and cutting the opening and closing stand-up segments that were similar to George and Gracie's harking back to their vaudeville days on their show. It didn't work. If anything, the show was worse for the changes. Later syndicated in reruns, the show still runs in various portions of the country.

Bud and Lou, despite the demise of their radio and then their TV show, continued to make films for Universal, but these were faint shadows of their funnier, earlier products. After meeting the mummy and nobody really caring, Universal dropped the team in 1955. In 1956 they made *Dance with Me, Henry* for United Artists, but it was a dud. It had been well over a year since their last film had been released and their hopes were duly smashed. They were having other troubles in 1956, the arguments over the years grating away at Lou more than Bud, and who was on first or who was on second didn't matter anymore. They never worked together again.

Bud more or less retired from performing and tussled with the Internal Revenue Service in a losing battle. He did little but try to cancel his debts until he teamed with Candy Candido, a "Colgate Comedy Hour" alumnus and comedian who switched from falsetto to a deep bass as his standard gimmick, and did some nightclub work in 1961. He also appeared on the "General Electric Theater," which along with "Playhouse 90," seemed to make a habit of using comics from split-up teams, and did his own voice in a cartoon series for Hanna–Barbera in 1967. Bud had had his share of physical ailments, being an epileptic and turning to alcohol as a dangerous antidote. He experienced a number of strokes in the late sixties and died of cancer in 1974 at the age of seventy-eight.

Lou was more active but did not last as long. As soon as the team split up he began doing a number of guest shots on "The Steve Allen Show." Even though the team's separation was friendly, especially in light of the ugly split up of Martin and Lewis, they did have some rough spots that showed. As the years went on Lou objected to second billing and the traditional 60/40 split of straight man and comic (which changed when Lou demanded it). The tension due to their sliding popularity did not help the act. But their grievances, more Lou's than Bud's, were relatively normal for any ongoing partnership, whatever the nature.

Lou did a "G.E. Theater" prior to Bud in 1958 and he also did a segment of "Wagon Train." He went back to live performing in Las Vegas at the Dunes Hotel. Ironically, he was appearing in "Minsky's Follies of 1958," a similar title to the show that started the duo. His straight man was Sid Fields. This was Lou's last appearance on stage, doing the burlesque routines he and Bud had so adroitly made common knowledge through their films and TV show. Lou made his only solo film at Columbia in 1959. *The Thirty-Foot Bride of Candy Rock* was not a fitting swan song for Lou Costello. He died of a heart attack at a young fifty-two soon after the filming.

The little, fat man/boy with the checked coat, a too-small derby, and a tie that almost touched the floor was a good foil for the tall fatherlike con man with the pencil-thin mustache. Some of the elements are familiar: Oliver Hardy was fat, wore a too-small derby, and fiddled with his tie continually. Stan was thin, the opposite of his partner. Abbott and Costello took up the tradition of physical humor that Laurel and Hardy had patented and the Marx Brothers also used. But both Laurel and Hardy had defined characters that an audience could identify with; the Marx Brothers were all distinct, even with Zeppo being distinctly nondistinct. George Burns and Gracie Allen were not physical comedians but their onstage or on-camera personalities were complete and completely identifiable. Only a stand-up comedian who does a short routine can sustain lack of depth as a person. Even then, most modern stand-up comics have a definite attitude toward most subjects. If they are translated to a film, or a TV show, or a radio show, they need to have an in-depth character, as Gabriel Kaplan does in "Welcome Back, Kotter." Bud and Lou retained the simplest of characters; they refused to root deeper. That fact, added to the limitations of their dated material, led to their quick success and quick relegation to the level of Saturday morning reruns. Their humor was too much like a cartoon. Abbott and Costello are represented in the late 1970s by a cartoon show. NBC has shown a study of the two comics' lives called "Bud and Lou" that stars Harvey Korman (Bud) and nightclub comedian Buddy Hackett (Lou). Hackett had been teamed once before in films with Hugh O'Brian in a 1954 movie *Fireman, Save My Child*. O'Brian and Hackett were contract players with Universal and filled in for Abbott and Costello when Lou fell ill in 1954.

If John Grant, their long-time writer, found agreeable places for their routines, even altering them and adding to them, he did not complicate their images. Their images needed that complication. Abbott and Costello have some bits that will outlast any one person. "Who's on First" is probably the most well-known comedy routine in the world. "Mustard," in which Bud convinces Lou that his not eating mustard on a hot dog will cause much of the world hardship, is still very funny. The problem is that anyone with good comedy timing could do those routines. Many did variations before Bud and Lou, like veteran vaudeville team Wheeler and Woolsey's map routine and their "Who's on First" bit, "The Baker Scene."

In a world that needs a laugh, it is difficult to say that Abbott and Costello were second-rate burlesque comics. They were first-rate burlesque comics. But a complicated world wants more than burlesque, more than word plays. They last for a time and are gone, as Abbott and Costello are gone.

CHAPTER **5**

Anything Goes, Everything Goes (Martin and Lewis)

DEAN MARTIN: We'd do anything that came to our minds.
JERRY LEWIS: I get paid for doing what children are punished for . . .

Most comedy is based on the common denominator of language. All comedy teams, before or after silents, have their roots in some form of verbal routine. As a result, they all improvised to some degree: Laurel and Hardy, while shooting a film or when trying out new material on the road, before live audiences prior to using it in a movie; Bud Abbott, countering asides thrown in by Lou Costello in their burlesque days or their days before the cameras; the Marx Brothers, actually germinating their madcap style prior to the big time by ad-libbing; even George and Gracie, on rare occasions, would add something new on the spot, even though they delved into impromptu ramblings the least of any of the big names.

If you had been present in Atlantic City in 1946 you would have experienced the most ad-libbed act of all time. A young Italian singer began his act, and as he softly crooned in a style molded on Bing Crosby and Perry Como a busboy dropped a whole tray of crockery in the middle of the room. There was an intense hush and then the singer and busboy exchanged a few words. The busboy tried to clean up the mess while the vocalist tried to continue the show. They shouted back and forth and became angrier. What ensued was pure madness. The singer and the busboy in their battling and arguing managed to trip waiters, pour water on customers and their cigars, hurl celery and assorted greenery all over, cut off men's ties, disrupt the band, monkey with the lights, con the customers into singing songs or bully them into joining a conga line, and generally wreak havoc and attack anything that was in sight.

The Italian crooner and straight man was Dino Paul Crocetti from Steubenville, Ohio. The busboy was Joseph Levitch, another comic from New Jersey like Bud Abbott and Lou Costello, only Joseph was from Newark. Dino and Joseph were destined to become the most highly paid, most important show-business entity of the fifties. They rose to stardom faster than anyone else had, commanded more money and fringe benefits than anyone else, and burned out quicker than even the wartime rise and postwar fall of Bud Abbott and Lou Costello in the forties and fifties.

Jerry Lewis (Joseph Levitch) was born in 1926 into a show-business family and was continually shuttled off to aunts, cousins, uncles, and Grandma Sarah while his parents played the small-time theaters and hotels in the Borscht Belt. Danny and Lea Levitch, who used the stage name of Lewis, did an act consisting of Lea accompanying Danny on the piano while he sang songs after the fashion of Al Jolson. Joseph nagged his parents into allowing him to debut at age five, singing "Brother, Can You Spare a Dime?" at the hotel they were currently booked into in the New York Catskill Mountains. He later became known as a crazy at Irvington High in New Jersey and whether in class, or as a cheerleader that competed with the team more than the opposition, he was nicknamed the "Id," which was short for idiot. Joseph got an "A" for clowning and madness but not for homework. He was even quoted later as having read only one book in his life, and that was not Dostoevsky or Dickens.

After punching an instructor in his first year of high school for making an anti-Semitic remark, Joseph left the schooling that he felt was slowing him up. He went through a series of jobs, including usher at Loew's State Theater in New York where he watched, learned, and copied from the great comics of the time like Milton Berle. He next got a job as a busboy where his parents performed and began developing his own act. The act was the easiest you could pick, consisting of comedy pantomime and silent mouthing or "lip-synching" (synchronization) to a record. There were a number of "dumb" acts that worked at that time and if you didn't sing or dance or have gags, or if you were new to performing in front of people, it was the simplest choice. You didn't have to talk directly to the audience or anyone else, you didn't have to memorize words so they were letter-perfect, and you didn't have to wait for laughs. That was the most important. If the laughs didn't come the next musical phrase would cover the loud silence.

Being born in Steubenville, Ohio, in 1917, the son of a barber, you might have a slightly different perspective on life than Joseph Levitch. There are more similarities between Lou Costello and Dean Martin (Dino Crocetti) than between Dean and his later partner, Jerry Lewis. Like Lou, Dean boxed, was from a Catholic family, and his father was an Italian immigrant. Dino was exposed more to gambling than to show-biz glitter. Steubenville ("little Chicago") was known, like Cincinnati at the time, chiefly for gambling and bootleg whiskey.

Dino horsed around at Grant Junior High but it was more to impress girls and his buddies than to get attention like Jerry at Irvington. Jerry would make a face or fall down for a cocker spaniel. Dino, like Jerry, quit school in the tenth grade, embarking on varied short-lived careers: he was a milkman, a gas "jockey," a steel mill worker, and an amateur boxer (welterweight) winning twenty-four of thirty bouts and finally working up to $10 a fight. Dino was definitely against this much exertion and the paltry sums he made, so he began running bootleg liquor. His parents caught him and he found himself the perfect niche for an easygoing guy. He began working at the Rex Cigar Store, a notorious local gambling house.

He started earning good money, about $100 a week with under the table antics, and was settling into his life. He exercised his baritone voice when socializing with the boys at Reed's Mill or Walker's Nightclub. Ernie McKay, a bandleader, heard Dino one night and offered him fifty bucks a week to join his band as a singer. Dino was making twice that, so he turned it down. The story has it that he was "influenced" by his friends at the Rex Cigar Store, guys like Lighthorse Harry, to join McKay's band in Columbus, Ohio. He began singing with McKay and in a short time was offered a raise by another bandleader from Cleveland, Sammy Watkins.

Back in the Catskills, Joey got his record act together and did it at Brown's Hotel, where his folks worked and he continued as busboy. A comedian on the bill, Irving Kaye, took Joey under his wing and got him a job at a theater in Hoboken. The result was that both Joey and Irving were fired from Brown's. Irving became Joey's manager and the record act went over so well in Hoboken that Joey committed himself to a career as a comic and changed his name to Jerry Lewis.

His next receptions were not very good and he didn't take to booing all that well. With help from older, tried performers, he persevered. His father managed to finagle Jerry an agent, Abbey Greshler, and the agent got him his first decent booking—as an emcee. Jerry panicked. He wasn't ready to say real words in front of live people. Greshler forced the point and Jerry did it, much to the dismay of the audience. But it was 1944 and a lot of people were playing World War II instead of theaters, so he wasn't fired. He even played the Glass Hat in New York and worked up from the $7 a week in Hoboken to $80 a week.

The booking agent for Sammy Watkins' band was an agent for MCA (Music Corporation of America), one of the two or three large theatrical agencies. He booked Dino—now Dean Martin—into the Riobamba nightclub in New York, the same club where Frank Sinatra had just broken the house records and then took off for Hollywood and a movie contract. Dean did not erase Frank's memory, but he did manage to go to on-and-off bookings in the $200–a–week category. Many people felt that part of Dean's problem was his large nose. Dean borrowed some money and got a nose job.

In 1945 Jerry and Dean were both playing the Glass Hat, Jerry doing his record act and emceeing, Dean as the featured singer making $500 a week. They did not make a particularly good impression on each other. They next crossed paths the following year at the Havana–Madrid in New York, a club that catered to a Spanish-speaking clientele. Jerry was bombing, and in an effort to save face he asked the management and Dean if he could "fool around on the floor" after Martin had finished the main part of his vocal stint. Dean was an easy guy so he agreed, as did the management.

Jerry came in dressed as a busboy and dropped the first tray of dishes. Then he and Dean insulted each other while picking up the mess. At the next show the bit was spruced up. Jerry liked it so much he suggested teaming up but Dean rejected the idea. Their paths continued to cross on the nightclub circuit but they were definitely singles. Later that year, 1946, Jerry was playing Skinny D'Amato's Club 500 in Atlantic City and, again, bombing. Jerry called Lou Perry, an agent who now handled Dean, and asked for help; his own agent, Greshler, was not useful, for D'Amato held him responsible for Jerry's act. Perry made a deal for the two of them to play together with Jerry cutting out the records and doing only the busboy bit. The owner balked but figured nothing could be worse than what he was now stuck with.

They tried the crashing dishes again but there was no reaction. They started to look over their shoulders for a cement mixer but then the ice was broken. Sophie Tucker, who happened to be in the audience, thought the bit was funny and laughed in her large, deep voice. The rest of the house joined in. It was lucky for Martin and Lewis that they had used W. C. Fields' old bit at the beach that day. Jerry pretended to be drowning, Dean saved him, and when a crowd gathered for the cheerful outcome of the heroic deed they did a pitch for their show that night.

When the audience started to react, the chaos that became known as Martin and Lewis's trademark ran rampant.

Told in show-biz terms, Martin and Lewis's rocket to stardom was meteoric. In truth, they shot up from a few hundred dollars a week at the 500 Club to over a thousand in their next engagement. Their popularity, the demand for them, and their price accelerated rapidly in nightclubs but they did not become known to the general public for another three years. The really big time was a little way off but for two performers who were never sure where their next paycheck was coming from, most particularly Jerry, they were doing all right. From Atlantic City they moved to the Latin Casino in New Jersey, then on to Loew's State in New York. These were followed by Bill Miller's Riviera Club in New Jersey and the Chez Paree in Chicago.

Due to the nature of their physical, ad-lib act, they seemed locked into clubs. How do you move a free-for-all with no order into an ordered, plotted medium like movies where the real money lay? Even the Marx zanies worked within a plot line. There were also disclaimers about the originality of their material. Many of their bits, like the drowning come-on in Atlantic City, came from others, even if they added twists or changes to them. Other comics from Jack E. Leonard to Milton Berle, who would later accept their help, carped about their "borrowing" material. But the twosome continued to pack houses and get their first taste of security, a security that each lacked when performing on his own.

In 1948 they played the Copacabana in Manhattan, the nightclub equivalent of vaudeville's Palace Theater. They did two shows a night and a third show at the Roxy movie theater, bringing their take close to $15,000 a week. Their energy might be attributed to their age; Jerry was twenty-two and Dean was thirty-one, both of them young by show-business standards. Later that year they played *the* club in Los Angeles, Slapsie Maxie Rosenbloom's. The opening was attended by the Hollywood bigwigs. Hal Wallis outbid other producers, offering them a five-year, seven-picture contract at $50,000 a film. They were not stars but supporting players in that first film, *My Friend Irma*, but they were the highlights of the Paramount picture. Their schedule was getting hectic for they were still playing clubs. Six months later *My Friend Irma Goes West* opened and they were quickly overtaking Abbott and Costello as the number one money-makers in the industry, soon to be voted the number one box office draw in the country in 1950 and 1951.

To take up any slack time in 1949 they sandwiched in radio appearances between their filmmaking and nightclub gigs. They did several of Bob Hope's radio shows, "The Big Show" with Tallulah Bankhead, and even managed an early TV appearance on "Welcome Aboard," one of the first television variety programs. This led to their own radio show, "The Martin and Lewis Show," which became a projection of their club act. It was not well received but somehow managed to survive for a few years. Their humor was raucous, visual pandemonium, and did not come across to mere ears, even with the efforts of two new writers who would later make them television stars: Ed Simmons and Norman Lear.

Despite their beginnings as a team, with Lewis being the low-paid, limited emcee and Martin the casual headliner, now Lewis was singled out as the mainstay while Martin was ignored or characterized as a hanger-on. In their first movie Jerry almost had a complete career halt, not being able to adapt to acting with prescribed lines and precise action. If Dean was wooden in front of the camera, Jerry was close to useless. But eventually they found a way of getting Jerry's undisciplined clowning filmed and, there too, he took the reviews away from Dean. This did not sit well with Dean and, even though he put up with it for years, it indicated the inevitable split the team would have ten years after they banded together.

As part of the contract with Wallis at Paramount, Martin and Lewis were allowed to make one film a year under their own auspices. In 1949 they made their first starring film *At War with the Army* under their York Productions title. It was released in 1950 and they were full-fledged stars at the top. As soon as they hit the zenith, both men seemed instantly to acquire money problems, with Dean taking the lion's share of debts. He owed everyone except Jerry, and that was because Jerry didn't have any money to lend. But despite these problems, their popularity soared.

With films and nightclubs conquered, they moved into TV in 1950 guesting on Milton Berle's "Texaco Star Theatre," which was the top show in the nation. They even stole the hour from the usually unshakable Uncle Miltie and were signed to do a new variety show called "The Colgate Comedy Hour," rotating star status with several other names (Eddie Cantor, Abbott and Costello, Donald O'Conner—and, for a short time, Fred Allen).

When they started the show it began as all Martin and Lewis ventures—haphazardly. The difference was that Jerry

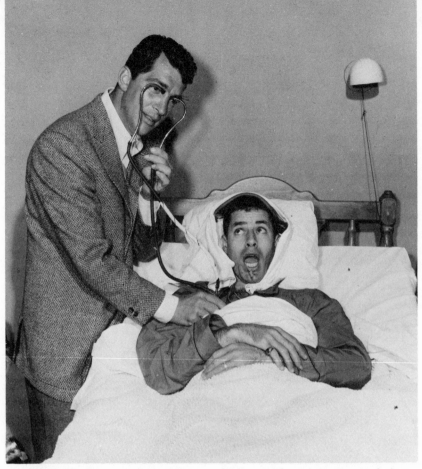

Dean Martin (l.) attempting to find out why Jerry Lewis (r.) still gets all of the gaglines even when he is ill (1953). (*Wide World Photos*)

had seen "Ford Star Review" and insisted on the scripters of that show, Ed Simmons and Norman Lear, as writers for their trek to TV, as he also did for their radio show. Lear, of course, is one of the leading television writer-producers of the seventies with "All in the Family," "Sanford and Son," "Maude," and "Mary Hartman, Mary Hartman" just a few of his products. Simmons is a top comedy writer on various shows. The stage manager of the Colgate show was soon promoted to director and his name, Bud Yorkin, was linked with Lear on some of the above shows, forming another team and pointing the way toward the move to writing of the later comedy teams. Yorkin now produces and writes independently. "The Colgate Comedy Hour" augmented Martin and Lewis's fairly large film audience and they eclipsed Abbott and Costello as the highest-paid act in the business.

Just to quell any doubts about their number one position, they played the Paramount Theater in New York in 1951 and broke the house record (set by Frank Sinatra), doing almost $300,000 in two weeks and getting an unheard-of salary of nearly half that amount. They did six shows a day, but even so, these were blockbuster figures. Martin and Lewis had accidentally found the power of the new television medium. They became "instant" stars known to everyone almost simultaneously.

The films continued to bring in heavy receipts with *That's My Boy* and *Sailor Beware* in 1951 and *Jumping Jacks, Road to Bali* (co-starring with Bob Hope and Bing Crosby), and a film from Columbia (as opposed to their parent studio Paramount) called *Hollywood Fun Festival* in 1952. *Sailor Beware* was a remake of two earlier films and was partially saved by John Grant, who wrote most of Abbott and Costello's bits in their films. The fact that Dean and Jerry made films that grossed a lot did not mean that they made good films. But as their price and popularity rose, Dean became more and more disenfranchised with being a third cousin instead of a full partner. He was either unmentioned or slighted in reviews and columns and even the film and TV writers geared their work to Jerry. Lewis was interested in the production aspects of films: writing, directing, cinematography, music, and so on. Dean, given the back-seat situation he was put in, simply wanted to play golf more and more. He would linger on the green until it was mandatory for him to come to the studio, shoot his boring straight lines, and occasionally croon a "post Crosby baa" ballad when it came that time in the script. The inevitability of their success was also looking like the inevitability of their break-up as a team.

As opposed to mild gossip, definite rumors began in 1954 that they were going to part company. Jerry was getting more and more pushy and, fashioning himself as the continuation of Charlie Chaplin, began to usurp everyone's prerogatives—producers, directors, writers, composers, conductors.

Prior to 1954 they had made *The Stooge, Scared Stiff* (one more comedy chiller film), *The Caddy,* and two more films. They actually did have a major rift during the filming of *Three-Ring Circus* in Phoenix. But for one reason or another—fear of going it alone, need of money—they stuck together. There was a truce of sorts, and they finished four more films, including *Artists and Models.* Their last film together was the easily forgettable *Hollywood or Bust.*

Their next scheduled film was *The Delicate Delinquent,* and finally Dean just refused to play the straight, lackluster cop to Jerry's starring role (Darren McGavin did the role). The split was official and they played their last contracted date at the Copa, breaking house records, in July 1956. The predictions were universal, as they had been all along, that the dynamic Jerry Lewis would make it big and that the innocuous Dean Martin would become a down-and-out saloon singer. The initial results look as if that would, indeed, be the case. Both men were insecure about what to do and whether they could manage alone. Jerry filled in for Judy Garland in Vegas, gaining confidence, and then filmed *The Delicate Delinquent,* which was a huge success. Dean did *Ten Thousand Bedrooms* for MGM and bombed.

Jerry went back to clubs and he was a winner. Dean was out of work for a while. Jerry got his own TV variety show in 1958 and it ran to the early sixties. He also signed a $10-million film contract with Paramount and proceeded to make his chaotic, childish formula films: *The Geisha Boy, The*

Errand Boy, Cinderfella, Visit to a Small Planet, (a mutilation of Gore Vidal's play), and *Boeing Boeing,* to name a few. These films appealed, as Abbott and Costello films do now, to children. The difference is that the A & C films were made twenty years earlier and are from a simpler, more naïve time. Adults found the humor in Jerry's movies sophomoric and crude—at times even insulting and brutal. Jerry even began cutting records in what has been called a "yapping and nasal" voice. However, his first disc sold a million copies.

Dean had his first million-seller record "That's Amore" almost by accident. It was part of the score of their film *The Caddy* and Dean didn't like it; he recorded it when the studio applied pressure. He had two more big hits but they were long gone when he split with Jerry in 1956. While Lewis was turning himself into a one-man studio, Dean put an act together and played the Sands Hotel in Las Vegas in 1957. Unofficially, Ed Simmons helped him put the show together, although it is alleged that Dean did it on his own. Prior to his going solo again, Dean had always been a rather bland straight man, his only character being a half-hearted pursuer of women who got Jerry out of scrapes and, when there was a pause in the action, sang Italian ballads. He now began to develop a distinct character of his own. He utilized his natural, relaxed, don't-give-a-damn attitude and incorporated the half-drunk booziness of earlier types like Phil Harris.

The character was immediately accepted by the audience and Dean shocked everyone with a smash at the Sands. He wasn't running the whole show the way that Jerry was but then he didn't want to. He landed a good role in a 20th Century-Fox film, *The Young Lions,* and starred with Montgomery Clift and Marlon Brando. He received the first really good critical notices he had ever gotten in the eighteen films that he had made to date.

Dean had known Frank Sinatra vaguely, but they really became friends during the filming of *Some Came Running*. He was accepted as a member of Sinatra's "Rat Pack" and next shot *Ocean's Eleven*, with a cast composed of that same Rat Pack. By the early sixties Dean owned a part interest in two hotels, made almost $300,000 per picture and $50,000 a week in Vegas. He was also doing well as a recording artist.

Both Dean and Jerry had made it alone. No other team has quite accomplished this. Of course, some didn't try. Laurel and Hardy never really split up. Only one of the Marx Brothers, Groucho, made it on his own. George Burns has become a star on his own, but it was many years after Gracie retired and left the act.

Jerry's recordings were hit and miss, so he did not pursue singing as one of his major endeavors. With the cancellation of his TV show in 1961, he returned to grinding out his child-comedy spoofs. He took over "The Tonight Show" for two weeks and was well received, but Johnny Carson was destined to take over the show from Jack Paar. Jerry became more and more obsessed with doing everything himself. He directed, wrote, produced, edited, composed, conducted, danced, sang, acted, and mimed. Dean simply made money and moved from film to film, ranging from comedies (*What a Way to Go*, Neil Simon's *Come Blow Your Horn*), to Westerns (*Durango, Rio Bravo* with John Wayne), to musicals (*The Bells Are Ringing*), to action films like *The Silencers*, which inaugurated the Matt Helm series that he starred in. He even started doing disaster movies like *Airport*.

In 1965 Dean agreed to do a television show. Since the days of "The Colgate Comedy Hour" he had pointedly avoided doing a regular television show because he just didn't want to rehearse and turn out a show every week. It was too much work and cut into his golf. In 1963 Jerry had started another TV stint, this time a talk show. But despite a large budget, the show was a flop and was replaced by "The Hollywood Palace." Dean hosted a few segments of "Palace" and that led to "The Dean Martin Show" in 1965. The show, with Dean only flying in on the day that it was shot, rehearsing, and then doing it, lasted a long time in terms of TV variety shows. It eventually evolved into a "roast" format and survives in the late seventies as a once-in-a-while special.

The roast was borrowed from a performers' club called the Friars. One man is chosen to receive accolades from friends and fellow performers; the twist is that instead of accolades he receives 90 percent humorous insults and 10 percent compliments. The honored guest is, of course, allowed to respond after his "friends'" comments.

Dean became a bona-fide millionaire from the TV show and his asking price changed to $150,000 a week in Vegas, then soared much higher. His television appearances and films are rare. He just doesn't need to make them and doesn't want to. He is happy with his life, has time for golf and a new wife and is now mellowing in his early sixties.

Jerry, in his fifties, is less carefree. He has tried to make it in television on numerous occasions and simply cannot. His movies, although grossing good amounts until the late sixties, are now paling. He left Paramount after making *The Nutty Professor*. He then made three turkeys for Columbia: *Three on a Couch, The Big Mouth,* and *Don't Raise the Bridge, Lower the River.* Trying TV again in 1967 he managed to last two seasons. In 1970 he made a film for Warner Brothers (*Which Way to the Front?*) and he does guest appearances, occasionally hosting "The Tonight Show." His guesting on other shows is infrequent. He still does his annual telethon for multiple sclerosis.

Jerry has never seemed to recover from the split with Dean. Dean, on the other hand, seems to handle it fairly easily. The two men hardly speak, although Dean tries, even going so far as to plug one of Jerry's TV shows on his own hit show. There was a brief encounter on Eddie Fisher's TV show in 1958 but the two men have rarely spoken for twenty years. In 1976 Frank Sinatra appeared on Jerry's telethon and surprised Lewis by having Martin come out for a reunion. There was a strained look on Lewis' face, then they both embraced, but it was plain that Jerry would not allow himself to forgive and forget.

It is evident that of all the major comedy teams Martin and Lewis were the weakest, unless one considers the Three Stooges a major comedy team. Martin and Lewis lacked the wit and creativity of the Marx Brothers, the classic timing and vulnerability of Laurel and Hardy, the lovable character of Gracie and the easygoing talent of George Burns, even the sure-fire routines of Abbott and Costello. That is most likely why they burned out so fast; if they hadn't broken up, they would have jointly fallen into obscurity. The fifties was a time of not making waves and Lewis's craziness was a hit because it was against the grain, totally different from the norm. There was no other team capable of filling the gap left by Abbott and Costello. Hence, the success of Martin and Lewis.

CHAPTER 6

Tweedledum and Tweedledee vs. the Ogre, or Satire and Punishment (The Smothers Bros.)

A man playing George Washington, with Revolutionary uniform and white wig, is picketing ornery old King George of England. A British Redcoat spots him and shouts, "Keep this hippie off the streets or we'll lock him up for good." The man who is impersonating the father of our country complacently replies, "Yes, it's gonna be a great country—one nation, invisible, with liberty and justice for most of us."

The man playing Washington was Tommy Smothers.

Although America is the freest society the world has known, that does not mean that there is no resistance to certain ideas, nor to particular ways of expressing ideas. Political satire has always been held suspect by American audiences and critics, as the Marx Brothers found out when their film *Duck Soup* fell far short of their earlier successes. In other countries people are often jailed for expressing their opinions; in America they are not. But there is no law in this country requiring people to listen. Nor is there a law requiring that a person with a controversial idea must be given a public platform.

If the blandness, isolationism, and don't-make-waves attitude of the fifties were exemplified by Abbott and Costello

and the inanity of Martin and Lewis, the sixties were epitomized by the social and political satire of Tom and Dick
Smothers. There was a reaction against their brand of humor,
and Rowan and Martin enjoyed national fame for a while
as a result. Whether the negative reaction was from the public or from other sources is not clear. The public rarely shows
its true colors en masse. But the sixties were years of social
and political turmoil in America. The Vietnam war was caus-
ing dissension among various groups; young students dem-
onstrated on campuses and in the streets; and President Lyn-
don Baines Johnson chose not to run for a second term as a
direct result of this uneasiness.

By turning to satire, both political and social, comedy reflected this unrest. It was the first time comedy had been so
overt in many years. Lenny Bruce commented on religion,
sex, society at large, politics, and just about everything else;
he was harried, then silenced. Mort Sahl pointedly com-
plained about government in his comedy monologues. But
the comedians who carried the torch for the young point of
view, the team that most visibly, via television, criticized
the Establishment's institutions, was the Smothers Brothers.
They were chastized for their stand.

Other comedians have always made topical allusions to
the social temperament of the time and to the political cli-
mate. Bob Hope has been making barbed social comments
for years and Rowan and Martin went one step further than
Hope in making fun of the Establishment, the government,
and politicians. The difference was that Hope, with a usual
bias toward the Establishment, would hit both sides of the
issue and would never touch anything that was truly controversial. On their TV show "Laugh In," Dan Rowan and
Dick Martin hit everyone with equal value, or tried to, and
did it so quickly and concisely that most people were never
quite sure what was being criticized. Tom and Dick Smothers took a definite stand. That in itself is almost unique in

comedy. Chaplin made some definite points in his later work and, whether his views were right or wrong, was ostracized as a result. Hardly any of the other teams did more than entertain. That is all they and most other people felt was required or desired of comedy. The Smothers Brothers disagreed.

In 1968 Tom and Dick were quoted in the magazine, *The Nation:*

DICK: Our show is entertainment, but it has to have social comment. It can't be created in a vacuum.

TOM: Social satire has to be done within the bounds of art. If it isn't, it won't work. It is self-defeating. All the best art comes out of society itself. Now is the time of change [sic], and it is reflected in art.

Like Lenny Bruce and Mort Sahl, even though coming from a different point of view from either man, the Smotherses saw comedy as more than just laughing. They wanted to express their ideas, to say something, to achieve what some consider the highest aim of art: to teach as well as to entertain. The great Greek dramatist Aristophanes did it, Chaucer did it, Shakespeare did it, Jonathan Swift and Voltaire did it. Tom and Dick Smothers wanted to do it, too.

They most likely did not decide on these goals as a result of their upbringing. Thomas Bolyn Smothers the third was born in 1937 on Governors Island, New York City, and twenty months later his brother Richard appeared at approximately the same place. Whether at this early age they looked like "two lollipops with ears," as one reporter later described them, only their mother Ruth knows. But there they were with no comedy material, stranded on an army base where their father, Major Thomas Bolyn Smothers was stationed. By 1940 they had acquired a sister, Sherry. After the family had relocated to the Philippines where the major had been transferred, World War II erupted and the family was evacuated on the last ship back to the States. Major Smothers was captured on the peninsula of Bataan and died a prisoner of war.

The family wound up in Redondo Beach in southern California. The boys attended elementary school there and a military academy for a while. After graduating from high school, Tom went on to San Jose State College in northern California. He was an advertising major, which would seem ironic to later fans. Tom lured Dick to San Jose when he graduated from the twelfth grade and Dick, the more conservative of the two, was a business administration major. Dick worked his way through his sophomore year of college and Tom cavorted as an athlete, a cheerleader, and fraternity cook during his sojourn through half of his junior year.

Tom ran into a little trouble in his first fraternity by attacking some of the hallowed precepts that the Greek organization perpetrated on pledges. His social criticism begun, he was asked to leave. He also played the guitar and sang folk tunes—an important endeavor in college in the late fifties. Tom persuaded Dick to take up the double bass. Tom had organized a folk group called the Casual Quintet and he wanted Dick to be a part of the group. Dick took to the bass and they played frat parties and entered talent contests, finally getting their first professional gig at the Kerosene Club, a rathskeller near the college. They had a free supply of peanuts, all the beer they could drink, and a whopping $7 to split four ways.

The quintet recorded an album for Aladdin Records and promptly lost a member. As a trio they managed to get a booking in 1959 at the Purple Onion in San Francisco. The Onion was gaining a reputation for introducing folksingers and comedians and later became the hip place to play. The featured act on the bill was a flamenco dancer who, believe it or not, twisted his ankle before opening night. The trio offered to do a longer show but their lack of enough rehearsed songs forced the three to talk among themselves. Tom became the focal point by adopting the attitude of a ten-year-old with a penchant for practical jokes and a typically jealous attitude ("Mom always liked you best!").

The little boy character was engaging and done in a wily way that was totally unlike Lou Costello's dumb, whining little boy. Dick was a born laconic straight man. The humor worked and the young, hip audience found that they got more for their money: folk songs and laughs. One of the routines that evolved was Dick explaining to the audience that their next number was the well-known folk song "Michael, Row the Boat Ashore." Tom would smirk impishly and say, "Hey, Michael. You better get that boat back, you'll lose your deposit." It was not wit, it was not satire, it was not classic humor, but it was funny. As Tom was to say later, "Dick and I are attitude comedians. We work out of our own personalities." The audiences must have liked their personalities; their two-week gig turned into thirty-six weeks, breaking the record at the Onion.

The next year, 1960, with one more member gone, the two brothers played the Limelight in Aspen, Colorado. After their debut as a team, they went on to the Blue Angel in New York, which was the East Coast counterpart of the Purple Onion in that it was considered an "in" place and introduced new talent, especially comedians. Pat Harrington, Jr., an actor and comedian who now plays the know-it-all superintendent on Norman Lear's comedy series "One Day at a Time," saw the brothers and suggested that Jack Paar catch their act. Paar was then the host of "The Tonight Show" and was constantly on the lookout for fresh talent. Paar liked them and booked them on his show. The Smotherses made the transition to TV easily and became hot.

They guested fourteen times on Steve Allen's show and made other appearances on "The Garry Moore Show," "The Judy Garland Show," "The Andy Williams Show," "The Ed

Sullivan Show," and "The Jack Benny Show." They also did some specials. They squeezed in roughly sixty guest shots over the next few years. The television exposure enhanced their nightclub work and began a highly successful round of concert dates; they made $5,000 a night for the latter and $10,000 a week for the former.

Since the parting of Dean Martin and Jerry Lewis in 1956, no comedy team seemed able to fill the gap they left and make it as headliners. Noonan and Marshall tried but made a few films and then went on to separate careers. Rowan and Martin had been working for years but they did not really make it big until after the Smothers Brothers were on top and there was a backlash against the Smotherses' slanted, satirical humor. Bob and Ray were popular but in a limited medium: radio. Nichols and May were the first candidates, but they only did albums, TV guest shots, a few concerts and a Broadway show. Then they broke up, never having been exposed to the vast television audience for the saturation, once-a-week viewing. As a result of the Smotherses breaking new ground and touching subjects others had avoided, Rowan and Martin's "Laugh In" was given a go-ahead, but they were careful to offer an alternative that presented all points of view.

It was obvious that the Smotherses appealed primarily to the young, not Abbott and Costello's audience, but the teen-agers and under-thirty crowd. They also held the adults, at first. They seemed the antithesis of what the public came to know as the youth movement and hippies. No long hair, no beads, no Levi's. Tom and Dick wore suits and ties and had very short hair styles. Initially their humor was, for the most part, just jokes and fooling around. There were few attempts at social comment. The appeal to the young is what facilitated their numerous concert dates, including two shows at Carnegie Hall (1964 and 1965), the last one a sellout.

Things were going well for Tom and Dick when they suffered their first setback. In 1965 Four Star Television started filming the brothers' first TV series for CBS. "The Smothers Brothers Show" suffered from the usual corporate network idiocy. The premise of the half-hour was something more incredibly silly than "My Mother the Car," a series that boasted a car as the main character. A young Los Angeles executive (Dick) is beleaguered by the ghost of his dead brother (Tom). It seems that Tom had drowned and was now an apprentice angel. Commanded to help people in trouble, he ineptly attempts to become an official angel with the help of his brother.

The popularity of Tom and Dick managed to get them a reported viewing audience of roughly 35 million for their premiere. But those millions, along with the critics, left quickly and the show did not survive for long. Why the premise had originally interested the brothers is difficult to understand. Tom was quoted later as saying that they had let other people decide what they should do. Both he and Dick thought that the people running the show knew what they were doing. Obviously, they didn't. It was not what the brothers wanted to do. Even when Fred de Cordova took over as producer, there wasn't enough to salvage.

While they pondered just what their next big move would be, they joined Jimmy Durante, Agnes Moorhead, and others in a TV adaptation of Lewis Carroll's *Alice Through the Looking-Glass.* They played Tweedledum and Tweedledee.

CBS decided to do something that was more suited to the Smothers Brothers' style. "Bonanza," a Western series, had captured the Sunday night audience and the CBS counterpart, "The Garry Moore Show," did not compete well with the cowboys. The network decided to try Tom and Dick as a mid-season replacement in Moore's time slot. As the denizens of show business had predicted that Dean Martin would fail when Martin and Lewis broke up, they this time turned their usually murky crystal ball on the Smotherses

and figured they would bite the dust as victims of the Pon-
derosa cowpunchers. "The Smothers Brothers Comedy Hour"
laughed every one of their sixty minutes away from the
humbled Cartwright family. They were a smash. Then the
trouble started.

The show was a combination of singing and dancing, satire, sketches, and controversial humor. They had not struck
the more strident tone that the second season brought but
they were moving away from the innocent joking of the old
days. A lot of the material was simple.

TOM: Stay tuned for a trip around the world contest.
DICK: Wait a minute, there's no trip around the world contest.
TOM: I was kidding.
DICK: Then there's no contest?
TOM: Yes, there's a contest, but there's no world.

Nothing to shock in that. But as producers Saul Ilson and
Ernest Chambers played devil's advocate for the network,
things began to change.

The show began in February 1967 when times were changing quickly and radically. Student demonstrations had become prevalent. Feeling against American involvement in the
Vietnam war was at an apex. People were offended by
complacency, the hear-no-evil, see-no-evil, speak-no-evil attitude that had characterized the fifties. People were speaking out, getting involved, committing themselves to what
they believed was right, as opposed to sticking their heads
in the ground. Art began to reflect the times. Music was
transformed by the lyrics of groups like the Beatles and
later by Bob Dylan. Lenny Bruce and Mort Sahl had made
people aware that comedians could do more than just get a
laugh. But if Bruce and Sahl were too harsh for the always
conservative TV tube, the clean-cut, all-American Smothers
Brothers were not—for a while.

PAT PAULSEN (*a comic on their show*): Some people say our draft laws are inequitable, outmoded and unjust. These people are soldiers.

Here was something a little different. There were also constant attacks on LBJ, as President Johnson was known.

DICK: Just suppose you were in the President's place and he were in your place.
TOM: Unh-uh, I wouldn't trust him with *my* show.

Dick (l.) and Tom (r.) Smothers on their private gondola in the 70s. (*Courtesy Tom Smothers*)

You might be offending someone with that exchange too. It was obvious that President Johnson was a hawk (in favor of the continuation of the Vietnam war) and the Smotherses were doves (against the war). What they did was attack his position through humor.

If Tom and Dick were irreverent, the word most constantly applied to their show, they were also suit-and-tie-wearing, beardless, short-haired, nonviolent young men who had begun their show with guests like Bette Davis, George Burns, and Jack Benny. They were lauded in every publication, and even compared to Sid Caesar and the golden days of television when Caesar's "Your Show of Shows" was the biggest show on the air. It lasted that way for most of the first season, with the show being unequivocally the hit of the season and Tom and Dick fighting their ogre: the CBS network.

Most people thought they were crazy. They were stars at a young age, had a hit show, and commanded enormous amounts of money. It just wasn't enough. Dick, always the more conservative and imperturbable, followed Tommy's lead but it did not take over his life. He simply wanted to do what he could and live his life. Tom, the leader, became engrossed in the show, involving himself in the writing, set design, costumes, music, camera direction, all of it. He felt he had to make his views known. His views were in accord with the views of the young and of minorities. He was sick of doing "dumb, say nothing" comedy. Along with millions of others, he was shocked by Vietnam, the riots in urban areas of America and the assassinations of Martin Luther King, Jr., and the Kennedy brothers. He wanted to do something about the hypocrisy and brutality he saw around him.

The second season was a pitched battle from beginning to end. There were no guns, no planes, no bombs. There was no killing. But there was an all-out fight. CBS would censor the show and Tom and Dick would try to counteract the "editing," usually by employing radio comedian Fred Allen's old ploy: giving the censors a number of things Allen knew they would delete in the hope that what was left would get on the air. It occasionally worked. The show trod on dangerous ground: the war, the President's position, draft dodgers, drugs, gun control ("Let's preserve our freedom to kill"), and even censorship itself ("We are not against censorship because we realize there is always the danger of something being said"). The lines were drawn and, ultimately, no one won decisively.

When casualties were counted up there were three or four major skirmishes. Pete Seeger, a blacklisted folksinger, was allowed on—after a battle—but then his song was cut up. In a rare move the network allowed Seeger to return, lyrics intact. There were no more rare moves. Another folksinger, Joan Baez, was "edited" because she referred to her husband, who was serving time in jail for resisting the draft. Singer Harry Belafonte sang a song to background film of the violence at the Democratic National Convention in 1964. It was cut. A routine with Elaine May, formerly of the comedy team of Nichols and May, was dropped because it seemed obscene to the censor. Of course, the point of the routine was that words are not obscene, the way that people use words is what makes words obscene. And so it went on.

CBS would not give more than an inch and slashed like mad. Tom would not budge but had to, since he did not control even his own show, let alone the network. Somehow Tom and Dick worked out an agreement and signed a monumental $4.5-million contract for season number three. Three weeks later, three months before American astronauts walked on the moon, on April 4, 1969, "The Smothers Brothers Comedy Hour" was canceled by CBS. The ogre had won.

Tommy had even gone to Washington, D.C., before the cancellation to try to find out what the basis was for all of their censorship problems. Was it only the network? Yes, it was. Why wasn't "Laugh In" being censored? Because they also had John Wayne and Richard Nixon on their show? No one knew the answer to that one. It is known that Tom and Dick's show was the only one on the network that was required to fly complete tapes of each show to the New York headquarters of CBS for previewing in advance. Some of the material was questionable and Tom cut it himself, even though he might think it was not questionable. He deleted a bit by comedian David Steinberg that the network bigwigs objected to. The routine had a religious basis and, although cleared by the Catholic Youth Organization and other similar groups, Tom cut it to appease the ogre. It was too late. The ogre was not satisfied.

Tom and Dick had their freedom but, thanks to the ogre, they were unemployed, with no platform for their brand of humor. They had an offer from a Canadian television network to do a "Smothers Brothers in Exile" show emanating from Toronto, but they declined the offer. That would seem to defeat the whole point of what they were doing, or what Tom was doing; Dick was involved in other things almost immediately. The ogre wouldn't get to Dick. They did do a special for another network, NBC. In 1968, before they lost their show, they tried a short-lived show, the "Summer Brothers Smothers Show," which didn't work but got singer Glen Campbell started. But there was no summer show forthcoming now. They filed suit against CBS and in 1973 were awarded over $900,000 in a judgment against the network for breach of contract and copyright. But in the interim their fortunes were mixed.

They took another shot at a show on another network (ABC), but this version of "The Smothers Brothers Comedy Hour" was diluted by the attempt to appease the new network. The ratings were low and it lasted only a few months. They next tried to avoid networks altogether with "The

Smothers Organic Prime Time Space Ride," which ran in syndication. The half-hour series was a variety show that introduced new talent. Tom hosted and Dick occasionally co-hosted, but the show sputtered out quickly. They still played nightclubs like Caesars Palace in Las Vegas and Harrah's in Reno and they guested on some shows and specials. Then they began to go out on their own.

Tommy took to producing. He had produced the "Summer Brothers Smothers Show" and the series spun off from that, "The Glen Campbell Goodtime Hour." He also co-produced the Los Angeles debut of the rock musical *Hair* at the Aquarius Theater. In his first acting role, Tom played a young guy who was "dropping out" in a Warner Brothers' comedy *Get to Know Your Rabbit*. He then co-produced a political satire film, *Another Fine Mess*, starring impressionist Rich Little.

Dick took his frustration to the racetrack. His interest in racing cars had grown, and after the break with CBS in '69, he participated in fifteen sports-car races in Canada and the U.S., which included the entire U.S. Grand Prix circuit. He finished eighth overall and managed first in his class at the Sebring (Florida) endurance races. In 1970 he went to Europe and the Continental Championship series for Formula A cars, racing two Lotus T-70's for the Smothers–Wintersteen Racing Team. In 1972 he won at Le Mans in France and retired from racing (for the first time).

By this time Tom had gone underground to lick his wounds and assess the whole CBS experience. In 1973, after winning the court case against the network, he began doing a single at the Cellar Door, a small club like the Purple Onion, in Washington, D.C. Dick rejoined his brother and they began doing concerts and nightclubs. Their last attempt at a series was for NBC in January 1975. The third "Smothers Brothers Comedy Hour" didn't have the bite of the original. They had to deal with tight controls as before even though the temper of the country had changed. The show had a short existence. Through all of the skelter-helter of their network wars they had still managed to record eleven albums, three of them gold.

They made sporadic guest appearances on "Sonny and Cher" and on "The Dick Van Dyke Show" in 1976, and still did some concerts and nightclubs. Tom made his stage debut in Woody Allen's *Play It Again, Sam* at the Cherry County Playhouse in Michigan. Tom and Dick announced on "The Tonight Show" that they were going to break up the act officially in December 1976. The last appearance of the Smothers Brothers as a team was at the Aladdin Hotel in Vegas. It was beamed to television via cable.

Dick came out of racing retirement to compete at Sebring again in 1977 but his team had to leave the race. His real emphasis has been on cultivating the thirteen-acre vineyard on his thirty-acre ranch in northern California and living full-time with his wife, three children, parrots, cats, horses, goldfish, and boa constrictor. Dick has been seen on numerous game shows, including "Matchgame" and "Tattletales" and has toyed with the idea of hosting a similar show that would require one or two days of taping every week or so. He made his acting debut in August 1977 in Neil Simon's *Prisoner of Second Avenue*. The event took place at the same theater in which Tommy had begun his stage career the year before, the Cherry County Playhouse in Traverse City, Michigan.

Tom renewed his role in *Play It Again, Sam* in 1977 in Seattle, Chicago, and St. Louis. Earlier he had completed filming the Michael Caine motion picture *The Silver Bears*, co-starring with Cybill Shepherd and Louis Jordan. Both Tommy and Dick dabble in talk-show guest appearances and film, Tom recently appearing in the movie *A Pleasure Doing Business* with Phyllis Diller. Both brothers made it to Broadway in 1978 co-starring with Barbara Sharma in the musical *I Love My Wife*. But, they do not play brothers in the show and still maintain that they will not reteam as a comedy act.

Tom and Dick Smothers burned out almost as quickly as Martin and Lewis, although it was more like being snuffed out. They had lasted longer than the earlier team's ten years together and they get on well, but they remained at the top for a shorter period of time. Dick had never been as excited about performing as Tom and he seems content to work separately every once in a while. Tom, who is divorced and lives alone, has fewer responsibilities and still pursues his career with zeal. Both had maintained earlier that two balding Smothers Brothers was not their act.

In the seventies, in the wake of Norman Lear's numerous series on TV, the Smothers show would probably not cause such a stir. One of their biggest gaffs with the network was over a routine that pointed up the insensitivity of many to the religious significance of holidays. The case in point was Easter.

DICK: Tommy, today is Easter Sunday. Do you know what Easter is actually all about?

TOM: Sure. It's the day Jesus Christ rose from his tomb . . .

DICK: That's right. I'm proud of you. I honestly didn't think you knew.

TOM: . . . and if he sees his shadow, he has to go back in again for six weeks.

Tom and Dick struggled over the issue of censorship at CBS. They lost the battle but they won the point. No other team has fought the powers-that-be for a cause. The rest were content to be funny, make money, and coast as long as the action would allow. But the Smothers Brothers wanted more and they put their career on the line to achieve it. Maybe that's what Tom and Dick think freedom is all about.

CHAPTER 7

Would You Buy a Used Car from This Bartender? (Rowan and Martin)

We are not trying to break down hypocrisy, as Lenny Bruce did; we are not trying to make a political point, as Mort Sahl does. The primary obligation we have is to entertain, and only after that to prick as many balloons as we can.

While Tom and Dick Smothers were matching verbal lances with the corporate windwills, another comedy team was fighting electronics with electronics. More in the mold of the classical stand-up comedy team, Dan Rowan and Dick Martin were unlikely candidates for the roles of social revolutionaries. If the Smothers Brothers looked conservative, Dan and Dick looked like your friendly neighborhood bank vice-presidents. In 1967 they were both in their mid-forties, tall and polished, and wore business suits and ties or tuxedos. They had been together as a team for fifteen years and had finally started to make it big. They held out for the kind of television show that they wanted to do and, inadvertently, made more profound social changes than Tom and Dick Smothers.

Dan Rowan was a used-car salesman and Dick Martin was a bartender. They met by chance, and fifteen years later became revolutionaries by chance. They had no plan for changing the American public and they professed no point of view other than that everything was fair game for kidding. But somehow they did change the social viewpoint of a lot of people. They merely wanted to be funny and to be successful. They accomplished both.

Dan Hale Rowan and Dick Martin were both born in 1922 —Dick in Battle Creek, Michigan and Dan in Beggs, Oklahoma. Dan's parents worked in a carnival and one story has Dan "starry-eyed" and onstage with them as soon as he could fake a tap dance. His parents died when he was eleven and he spent four years in an orphanage.

Both Dick and Dan finished high school and headed for Hollywood. Dick arrived a year or two later than Dan, by way of some stimulating work in a Ford assembly plant. The legend has Dan hitchhiking (like Lou Costello) to L.A. when he was nineteen. There was no doubt that both wanted some kind of career in show business. Dick began making headway as a writer for comedians like Ben Blue (an old-timer from vaudeville) and, in his early twenties, writing for a popular radio comedy of the time, "Duffy's Tavern." But he still had to rely on bartending for his main income. Dan wound up in the Paramount mailroom and, through diligence, worked up to junior writer, which meant he got to do all of the stuff that nobody else would do. With not a great amount of regret, Dan left being a junior for flying in World War II. After his tour of duty, he settled down to what he had decided was his passion—acting—and took theater arts courses in college.

Dick was tending bar in Slapsy Maxie's when Martin and Lewis were just making it big and played the club in 1946. He reasoned that throwing lettuce around was something that he might look into and he hooked up with comedian Artie Lewis. The team lasted about a month. Dick tried another act with comedienne Betty Miller, but it lasted an even shorter time, never getting beyond rehearsals and discussion.

Dan got married and left his acting lessons for a more esthetic pursuit. He became co-owner of a foreign car lot. Dick continued to tend bar and write on the side. In 1952 Tommy Noonan was doing fairly well as part of the comedy team of Noonan and Marshall (Peter Marshall, the host of "Hollywood Squares"). Noonan's wife was a friend of Dan's wife and he also knew Dick fairly well. What happened was that Tommy and Dan went into a bar in the San Fernando Valley where Dick was barkeep and Tommy introduced the two men. Dan had gotten bored with MG's and had started acting again; Dick was always on the lookout for a new partner. Nine days later Rowan and Martin did their "Shakespearean Actor vs. the Drunk" at Charlie Foy's Supper Club in L.A. It got a good word from another comedian on the bill, Joe Frisco. Frisco was famous for his stutter and used it to good effect in his act. He told Dick and Dan not to give up.

They have become known for the material that they tried out at Foy's club. After refinement, it became one of their classic bits of material. Dan, as the straight man, plays a Shakespearean actor who is constantly interrupted by a drunk, played by Dick. The routine flows easily. The character of their comedy was set from the start. Although they are more reminiscent of Abbott and Costello or Martin and Lewis than the Smothers Brothers or the Marx Brothers, they were quite different. They used no physical bits at all. Bud Abbott was constantly pushing and shoving Lou Costello around the stage or in camera frame. Dean and Jerry threw rutabagas at each other. Dan and Dick never touched each other. They look on their act as being "cerebral humor" and one of the reasons, besides dealing with Shakespeare as opposed to baseball, was this lack of vaudeville and burlesque roughhouse.

They also improvised their act and, twenty-five years later, that is exactly how they play any public appearance. Naturally they have stock routines that they use on some occasions: "Shakespeare vs. the Drunk," a doctor bit, a charades bit, but they don't always use premises that they have used before. Even when they use the proved premise, they vary the act. Although not a part of the formal schools of improvisatory comedy that proliferated in the sixties, like "The Second City" and "The Committee," they are one of the few teams that has made it big by improvising not as characters but as themselves. The Marx Brothers developed their act by improvisation and they continued to ad-lib in vaudeville, on Broadway, and in their films. But that was from an earlier time and the type of improvisation was much different and quite often physical in nature. Lou Costello ad-libbed on occasion. Martin and Lewis ad-libbed less than they admitted to and, when they did, it was quite often a stock line or a chair in the mouth. Jerry was quoted in *American Film Magazine* in 1977 as saying, "The spontaneity that looked like insanity was very well planned." Dan and Dick just stood there and talked. And it was funny. Today they may not see each other for months. They arrive on the day of their appearance, say hello and exchange pleasantries, then they go out on stage and talk.

Dan had some problems taking on the role of straight man because he thought of it as number two in a two-man show. But he soon accepted the straight man's importance—Dick was not as funny without Dan. Dan and Dick talked to each other, rather than to the audience. If Dick was "loose," Dan was described as a "rock" by Dean Martin. Dick could go off the walls because Dan pulled him back.

Dan and Dick took their act to various places in Los Angeles and other glamorous areas like Hobbes, New Mexico, and Hymie's cocktail lounge in Albuquerque. Eventually they began to get better bookings: the Chez Paree in Chicago, the Copa and the Latin Quarter in New York, and the Coconut Grove in Los Angeles. They were always heavily overshadowed, as most performers were, by Martin and Lewis.

Their first big break came the same year (1956) that Dean and Jerry split up. Walter Winchell, who had an enormous amount of influence, saw them in Miami and praised them in his syndicated column. Their club dates improved and they moved on to Vegas, Reno, and Tahoe, but only in the lounges, not in the main rooms. In 1957 they signed a contract with NBC, but there was a mutual parting of the ways by 1960. They didn't feel that the network was exposing their act properly; you cannot become stars by doing six guest shots on variety shows every year or so.

They also made a film that year (released in 1958) for Universal International studios. *Once Upon a Horse* was an attempt at a Western spoof but, according to Dick, it was subtle humor done before the days of the tongue-in-cheek humor of the "Maverick" television series. In 1960 they made their first album, "Rowan and Martin at Work," but it too was not anywhere close to a million-seller gold record. They continued playing clubs and, later in the sixties, they recorded their second album "The Humor of Rowan and Martin." Dan and Dick seemed fated to play clubs and lounges.

Then producer Greg Garrison "inked" them (show-business jargon for signing a contract) to be the summer replacement for Dean Martin's television show in 1966. They came out number one in the ratings race that summer and the network approached them for another contract. This time they balked. They did not want to do a straight variety hour, which is what was planned for them. They had definite ideas about the kind of show they wanted to do and it took some time to convince the network and bring it around. They went to two producers, Bob Banner and Garrison, but neither went for the concept. Finally they latched onto producer George Shlatter and "Rowan and Martin's Laugh In" was born.

There has been a great deal of controversy about whose idea the series was. The establishment of credit is significant because the show was perhaps the most singly innovative production of the decade. It has changed a lot of television fare and the audience's attitude, by its example. Commercials had begun to use quicker, cinematic techniques by 1967 but they were in a different style. Their object was simply to sell. The object of "Laugh In" was to make people laugh. What came about was Shlatter and the network claiming the idea for Shlatter and, to some degree, co-producer Ed Friendly. Dan and Dick claimed the idea for themselves. Shlatter had been touting a fast, quick-cut comedy series for a while, but when he first came to the comedians to discuss a show for them he talked about a special utilizing animation and animals. Rowan and Martin told him about their concept and he went along with it, after asking and getting 50 percent of the action.

The argument seems to be easily solved by the fact that according to Dick Martin, Dan and Dick had shot a show with a similar format to "Laugh In" five years earlier for a local station in San Francisco. But after the inception of the network show, its instant success, and the ensuing bickering, there were hard feelings that eventually led to Shlatter's leaving the series. Finally, the partners signed over the full rights to Shlatter ". . . with the stipulation that he remain off the set for two years."

After much cajoling and before the ownership war, the network (NBC) agreed, with trepidation, to do a pilot of the show that the comedy partners wanted. The special of "Rowan and Martin's Laugh In" aired September 1967. NBC, still not convinced, decided to replace a spy show that appealed to a young audience ("The Man from U.N.C.L.E.") with the new comedy series. It premiered in the NBC line-up in January 1968. Within three months the show was in fifth place in the ratings and it finished the season in first place. The competition was the number one show ("Here's Lucy") and the number three series ("Gunsmoke").

Unlike shows oriented toward satire like the Smothers Brothers and "That Was the Week That Was," "Laugh In" was simply intent on making fun of everything and anything. There were no favorites, no special points of view, no dwelling on social evils. The show was so fast that you could miss thirty jokes in an hour and not be aware that you had missed anything. Dick Martin baldly states, "We were the first show to ever use television as a visual medium. Up until then, Milton Berle was televised vaudeville [as were Abbott and Costello]. The others were televised radio."

Zoom-in close-ups, blackouts, quick cuts, slow motion—all the camera tricks that could be thought of were used. The show was compared to the pioneer work of Ernie Kovacs (a comedian, director, writer who experimented with extraordinary visuals and camera techniques in the fifties) and *Hellzapoppin'*, the no-holds-barred revue of vaudeville team Olsen and Johnson. On "Laugh In" Dan and Dick were the hosts and did an opening and closing routine that was usually intercut with other bits. They then returned to do various segments with the rest of the cast, a conglomeration of funny, bizarre kooks who portrayed themselves, characters, or animals and told one-liners, old jokes, new jokes, did quick, crazy skits, danced, sang, hopped, jumped, and generally made delightful fools of themselves. They fell through trapdoors, took pies in the face, marshmallows to the body and water in the pants, sat on collapsing chairs, crashed through walls, and performed everything else that had been

Rowan (l.) and Martin (r.) being told that George Schlatter had decided not to produce "Laugh In" in the last two seasons. (*Courtesy Dick Martin*)

used in vaudeville and burlesque, adding twists of their own. It all added up to the ten stooges.

The comedy writers for the show turned out more than three hundred jokes a week. The output was then cut to something over two hundred to fit into the fifty-three minutes of comedy that the commercial time left open. The cutting on the show was a stupendous undertaking, employing four men at one time. The normal hour on a variety series had roughly twenty-five or thirty cuts while "Laugh In" had somewhere in the area of 250, or whatever amounted to a cut for every joke. In the late 1970s this number has been superseded by the thousand editing cuts made in what is supposed to be a "live" show: the Dean Martin roasts. Added to that, the outakes that weren't used were kept for future shows, making the editing job the most difficult in TV or anywhere at the time. Art Steiner, the editor, and his staff, earned a well-deserved Emmy after the first season.

A possible script for the show might go something like this:

DICK: I don't look on them as dirty movies. I look on them as training films.

   Cut to:

JOHN WAYNE: Sock it to me, Pilgrim.

   Dissolve to:

HENRY GIBSON: A myth is a female moth.

   Cut to:

SAMMY DAVIS, JR: If I have one life to live, let me live it as a blond.

   Cut to:

JUDY CARNE Sock it to me! *(Judy is doused with water.)*

   Cut to:

DAN: News of the Past: 1793. On returning to Moscow today, the Czar and Czarina declined to discuss their honeymoon. But it was noted that he called her "Catherine the Great" and she called him "Ivan the Terrible."

   Cut to:

RICHARD M. NIXON: Sock it to *me*?

The names of the stock company that backed up Dan and Dick varied over the years, but the nucleus was comprised of Arte Johnson (the dirty old man and the German soldier—"Veeerrry interesting!"), Ruth Buzzi (the ugly lady harassed by the dirty old man), Goldie Hawn (the dumb blond), Henry Gibson (the minister and the poet), Jo Anne Worley (the loud-mouthed opera singer), Garry Owens (the old-time announcer), Judy Carne (the British "Sock it to me" girl who was always being deluged with one thing or another), and Larry Hovis (assuming various characters). The guests ran from Bob Hope to Billy Graham, Kirk Douglas to Richard Milhous Nixon.

The show won four Emmys in its first season and since it was a mid-season replacement, there were only fourteen shows. Over its six-year run "Laugh In" amassed almost as many Emmys as Walt Disney, who had nearly fifty.

Dick and Dan continued to do clubs while the show was on and particularly during the summer hiatus from filming, when filming is done for one season and has not started on the next. For two years they took most of the "Laugh In" cast out on concert dates doing fairs, sports arenas, and theaters-in-the-round. Dan and Dick always tried to take along another team as an opening act (Skiles and Henderson, Gaylord and Holiday) whenever they played. They wanted no Martin and Lewis image. Besides playing dates, the "Laugh In" crew, along with Rowan and Martin, recorded two albums of bits from the show.

"Laugh In" was innovative in many ways. It utilized the visual aspects of television to the most thorough extent to date. If you left your TV set during "Laugh In," you missed about fifteen jokes and many of the later ones in the show were based on things you had missed. Even if you heard what was going on, you still needed to see it to understand it. Just listening was not enough as it usually was with dramatic or variety series or even the usual comedy series. Generally the critics liked the show, but some did harp on the sophomoric humor. But then many things that are funny are, indeed, sophomoric. The show was not as relevant (a big word in the sixties) as the Smothers and TW3 ("That Was the Week That Was") but "Laugh In" was not attempting to be relevant. They did manage to criticize a lot of things, however. A ticker-tape running along the bottom of the screen might say "LBJ [President Johnson] Reviews U.S. Troops—in Canada." Someone would emerge from a haze of smoke and quip, "Of course I save cigarette coupons. How else do you think I got this swell iron lung?" A Southern colonel with mint julep, Panama hat, string tie and goatee stands at attention while black comedian Flip Wilson points and harangues, "How much am I bid?"

The jabs were balanced between liberal and conservative, right and left, and, as a result, the show had a long life. After the Smothers Brothers led the way and then succumbed to their unilateral point of view, "Laugh In" took over and bilaterally changed the limits of TV. As a consequence, a great many of the show's viewers were also changed. Tom and Dick Smothers really couldn't figure out why the censors were so heavy on them and so light on Dan and Dick's show. Both shows were known as "taboo-busters," and both changed social mores by using ideas and words that had never before been exposed to that many people on the tube. The Smotherses went for ideas and pursued them in detail. Rowan and Martin never spent time on anything and did not fall victim to the censor's wrath as often. But "Laugh In" was the first show to use the word "pregnant" on the air; previously, pregnancy was referred to by the euphemism "expecting." It wasn't a monumental step forward for mankind but it did loosen up the simple exchange of ideas. How did they get away with it?

The answer is manifold and certainly not complete. First, there was so much material crammed into the show's fifty-three minutes that it was hard to decide for sure whether something had gone too far. If something had gone too far, nobody was sure who it insulted. With most of the camera techniques and nonstop words crashing past your eyes and into your ears at approximately ten seconds for each joke, it was difficult to discern anything except whether it was funny or not. If you didn't laugh, there was another joke or bit right behind the last one, and another, and another. There was no time to reflect. You either laughed or took a breather to prepare for the next laugh.

Secondly, the show had a resident censor who went over every script before it got to camera and was present during rehearsals and tapings. The censor zeroed in on religion and sex as the areas to be touchy about, leaving political issues pretty much alone. "Laugh In," like Tom and Dick Smothers, put in jokes that would not clear the censor just to assure their getting the ones in that they wanted to be seen on the air.

Thirdly, Paul Keyes, the head writer whom Dan and Dick had insisted upon for the show, felt that they towed a close line between suggestive (blue) jokes and out-and-out dirty humor. Whatever the reason, the show lasted through the 1973 season and started a new life as a series of specials—without Dick and Dan—in 1977. The new series was George Shlatter's "Laugh In," due to the parting of the ways between the producer and the comedy team.

After the success of their TV show, Rowan and Martin signed a three-year picture contract with MGM. Along with "sock it to me" and "veeeerrrry interesting," "you bet your sweet bippy" had become a well-known phrase from "Laugh In." Their second film, the first after their huge success, was a horror spoof entitled *The Maltese Bippy*. All comedians have turned to a horror satire at one time or another. But all the hidden jewels, dead bodies, werewolves, and monsters could not make *Bippy* a hit. Another film, *The Money Game*, was planned but it was never shot. Nor was the third film.

After the series went off the air Rowan and Martin continued to do concert and cabaret dates. They both had become rich men from the show and were not unhappy when the show went off the air. After the fifth year they felt that there was nothing new to say, but the network made them an offer that they couldn't refuse. After the '73 season the ratings were down, as they had been for a while, and the network saw the light, dropping the show from its schedule.

Dan and Dick are now content to meet a few times during the year and ramble on about meaningless, funny things in front of an audience. The television Rowan and Martin is quite distinct from the live R & M. It is impossible to capture on paper what they do live. If you do capture their exchanges, it just isn't as funny as the real thing. But a John Wayne special will serve as an example:

DAN: Thank you, ladies and gentlemen. What's his name and I are delighted to be here tonight to honor one of the great personalities of all time . . .

DICK: Thank you.

DAN: John Wayne. . . . A man who has thrilled millions in such great films as *Back to Bataan.*

DICK: Shirley.

DAN: *The Flying Leathernecks.*

DICK: Madeline.

DAN: *Sands of Iwo Jima.*

DICK: Clara.

DAN: Dick, I'm talking about great battles in the movies.

DICK: So am I. . . . Shirley, Madeline, Clara.

DAN: I'm talking about John Wayne. He's big enough for two men.

DICK: So was Clara.

Although the public is not as aware of Rowan and Martin because of their infrequent TV appearances, their 1977 schedule included a special and three live dates in Miami, New Orleans, and New Jersey; '78 was about the same. Dan has decided that his twenty-five years with partner Dick have earned him some free time and he is somewhere in Florida, where he now lives. Dick makes an occasional commercial and both of them do talk shows—separately. The only times they have appeared together on television since "Laugh In" went off the air was a guest shot on "The Carol Burnett Show" and on an occasional special. They only did the Burnett show to pay back a debt they owed Carol for her guesting on "Laugh In."

Dick directed and wrote for "The Bob Newhart Show." He is a friend of Bob and Artie Price at MTM (Mary Tyler Moore Productions), which produced Newhart's show along with numerous others. He was asked to direct one segment, then another, and advanced to a minimum of eight shows a season. Dan and Dick both do TV and print commercials, perform every once in a while, and Dan has become the "almost" tennis amateur of Florida while Dick moves on as a director on "The Waverly Wonders," starring Joe Namath and hosting game shows since the Newhart show went off the air.

Dan Rowan and Dick Martin have an engaging intimacy and rapport with each other on stage that no other team can claim. Most teams address the audience directly, playing on their response: Abbott and Costello, Martin and Lewis, the Smothers Brothers, George and Gracie, and so on. There is a minimum of this kind of byplay in R & M's work. The audience feels as if they are overhearing two guys "chew the fat," one of the men (Dick) being much slower than the other. They have no interest in changing society. Other than characters in movies or TV series, there seem to be two schools of comedy since the agitation of the sixties. The comics that, at least to some degree, require that you laugh *and* think (Lenny Bruce, Mort Sahl, Nichols and May, the Smothers Brothers, Richard Pryor, George Carlin) and the majority that Rowan and Martin belong to that just want to entertain you (David Brenner, Johnny Carson, Don Rickles, Stiller and Meara, Bob and Ray, Bob Hope).

Dan and Dick are from the old school of team comedy in that they just come out and talk. They seem content to do that and audiences seem content to listen and laugh. They have been together twenty-five years as a duo and don't see any reason to retire the act. They played the lowlife clubs and at a Royal Command Performance for the Queen of England to help the British Olympic Fund. They feel they have done what a team should do. But they may be seen on TV again. Dick candidly admits, "If someone comes up with enough money we will play Utah." Maybe even Guam.

PART II
The Renaissance

CHAPTER 8

The Hidden Comedians (Teams of the '60s and '70s)

Comedy teams were a staple of both English music halls and American vaudeville. Along with Dot and Dash (the dance team) and the jugglers (like W. C. Fields), along with the song-and-dance man and Princess Pazmezoglue and Her Cockatoos, along with the magician and, so it seemed, always after the dog act, there was a comedy team. But the new media—films, radio, television—seemed to bring about a decline in the number of comedy teams that made it big and even the number of comedy teams that existed. For a while, comedy teams seemed an endangered species; then they experienced a resurgence in the sixties.

A few comedy teams jumped from vaudeville and Broadway to silent films: Clark and McCullough, Wheeler and Woolsey. But disregarding the Keystone Kops as a team, Laurel and Hardy was the only successful comedy team in the silents.

There were radio teams that were well known, like Fibber McGee and Molly (Jim and Marian Jordan), but as radio was silenced, so were they. Amos and Andy (Freeman F. Gosden and Charles J. Correll) were even more popular on the air waves, but a new set of actors played them on the TV series of the fifties. Ozzie and Harriet were popular on radio and were much more effective on TV, but they were more of a family than a team. Their humor was molded by the ultimate television comedy technique: the situation comedy. The only radio team that really rivaled George and Gracie in the late '40s was the late Edgar Bergen and his wooden friend Charlie McCarthy, but as much as audiences liked to think of Charlie and Mortimer Snerd as real, they were always attached to their partner the ventriloquist.

The Marx Brothers became stars in vaudeville, then moved on to Broadway and finally conquered films. Abbott and Costello were the undisputed kings of burlesque and then found their medium in films. Martin and Lewis were show-stoppers in clubs and did well in sporadic TV appearances, but cinema was their medium, too. There were a few other teams when Martin and Lewis took over in the late forties but, except for Abbott and Costello on their way out, none of them made it as stars until Tom and Dick Smothers and Rowan and Martin became household words via television in the late sixties.

There were always some teams, often husband and wife, who played smaller clubs or resort hotels and made a living of sorts. But after vaudeville died in the early thirties, the number of teams began to dwindle. It was not until the sixties, more than twenty-five years later, that a number of comedy teams made headlines and became headliners. None of these teams made any headway in films. With the unique exception of Bob and Ray, radio had become by the sixties little more than music, news, and sports. The days of the big nightclubs, except for Vegas, Reno, and Tahoe, had long been over. What was left, after Martin and Lewis seemed to play out the last of the team comedy films in the mid-fifties, were television, concert dates, and record albums. In a few cases (Nichols and May, Bob and Ray) there were comedy revues on Broadway, without the attendant music with which the Marx Brothers had surrounded themselves. The salient point is that after a long drought there was a stream of comedy teams once more.

There was also a change in the consistency of the teams in the sixties and seventies. A social change began in the sixties allowing women more freedom. There were more women in comedy than there had been before. The only female member of a successful comedy team prior to the sixties was Gracie Allen; the only exceptions were Molly in radio's Fibber McGee and Molly and the short teaming of Thelma Todd with ZaSu Pitts and, later, Patsy Kelly with Todd in almost forty MGM film shorts during the early thirties. Sometime after 1960 it finally dawned on at least some people that humor was not a male prerogative. Women could star in their own series, tell jokes, and write jokes. But there has not been, to this date, a successful comedy team made up solely of women.

The rise and fall of the various media seemed to have an enormous effect on comedy and comedy teams. First there was only the stage: music hall, vaudeville, then burlesque and "musical comedy." Films, with the help of radio, eventually ended all of these except for musical comedy, which evolved from revues into a form that is definitely book- or plot-oriented, theater rather than a conglomeration of musical and comedy sketches. Radio began to eat away at vaudeville and burlesque and when films added sound in 1929, both stage shows and radio began to suffer. By the 1940s movies had definitely eclipsed live shows and were rapidly moving in on radio and nightclubs. Night spots had become very big during Prohibition and grew as vaudeville failed.

Television started in the late forties but did not come into its own until the mid-fifties. It changed everything. Radio was soon reduced to its present state of news, sports, and music, cutting out the soap operas, dramas, talk shows, game shows and comedy shows. In the late seventies there has been an attempt to revive some of the old dramas and mystery shows. Nightclubs had virtually disappeared by the late fifties and the early sixties saw the demise of all of the large clubs. Even movies began to falter when television took hold. There is still a desperate ongoing struggle in the film industry to keep up with the pervasiveness of TV. It is very possible that by the nineties there will be very few movie houses left.

In the sixties, after total immersion in the living room TV set, people particularly young people, wanted to get out and see things live. A new way of getting more people to see a live performance and, hence, making enough money to make it profitable, was concerts. These are usually one-night or two-night bookings, many of them near colleges and appealing to the under-thirty group, that pull in huge crowds. There are no nightclubs, no problems with serving drinks and food, no particular attention paid to decor—there are just 12,000 people seeing an act.

The sixties also saw the revival of another medium, as far as comedy was concerned. With the advent of rock and roll in the fifties, there was an enormous growth in the record business. There was also a transition from singles at 78 and 45 rpm to albums at $33\frac{1}{3}$ rpm. That growth in record sales continued into the sixties with the Beatles and the change from rock and roll to rock, hard and soft. Word albums, albums with people talking and no music, had never been big sellers. The comedy team of Mike Nichols and Elaine May changed all that in the early sixties. Many comedians have now sold millions of albums by just talking. These sales do not match the millions on millions sold by singing groups and soloists, but in the late 1970s, Cheech and Chong are outselling many rock groups.

The previously discussed two types of comedy exemplified by Rowan and Martin (make them laugh) and the Smothers Brothers (make them think and laugh) seem to be the major change in comedy and comedy teams that began in the sixties. In reality the changes were beginning to be felt in the late fifties. Bob and Ray had been doing their unusual sort of satire before the sixties and Nichols and May were doing their sophisticated "scenes" in the late fifties. Rowan and Martin were the holdovers from a totally different style. Although they did not do the slapstick, push-around bits that Abbott and Costello and Martin and Lewis did, they were definitely Dan Rowan and Dick Martin talking in a funny way. The Smothers Brothers, although innovative in moving on to comedy that commented on the times they lived in, were Tom and Dick singing and kidding around. Rowan and Martin did not do many sketches on "Laugh In"; Tom and Dick did do sketches on their TV show.

The new teams were hidden. You might know their names but they constantly changed character, voices, and attitudes. They were totally different people in totally different situations. Mike Nichols might be a British dentist, Jenna McMahon a nun who tap dances and Avery Schreiber a machine. These comedians were not themselves telling jokes, they were somebody else living a life much like the audience they played for. They just happened to be very funny at it.

One reason for this change is that many of them were actors first and comedians later. Many of them were involved with the various improvisation groups that popped up in the sixties, most of them emanating from Chicago. Doing an improvisation demands that you take on characteristics of a different person, obviously, as any good actor does, incorporating the parts of your own style that fit. The comedians were a product of television, which meant that they had a background in the fast moving style of the medium and an overabundance of information. "Hip" or "hep" was originally a musician's term that meant you were aware of what was going on, that you were not naïve. Television managed to make large numbers of people hip to many things. It reached millions at one time and changed the naïve to the sophisticated, at least in a limited sense. "Laugh In" capitalized on this knowledge in its quickness and its use of hip or in terms and references.

If anything characterizes the humor of the sixties and seventies, it is satire. The college-educated actors, raised along with television, criticized through their humor. They chose to satirize everything from courting and dating habits to the presidency. They attacked social hypocrisy and they made us laugh. Bob and Ray had been satirizing their own medium, radio, for years. Nichols and May concentrated on the college-educated middle class. The later teams found their own channels, with Cheech and Chong, the newest team, gearing their jokes to young people, their music, their pursuits.

With the return of many teams, it is necessary to concentrate on a few, the more important ones or the most indicative ones. Allen and Rossi played Vegas and clubs across the country. The team did various guest shots on TV in the sixties as well, but they were a product of the old school, never rising above a lukewarm attempt at Abbott and Costello. Skyles and Henderson do an act similar in tone to the Smotherses in that they appeal to a college crowd, but that crowd belongs to the folksinging fifties and early sixties. There were other teams that banded together and disbanded or, in the trend of the seventies, turned to writing rather than performing. The teams discussed are either innovators or, in one way or another, exemplify the evolving trends in comedy teams through the late seventies.

Your Friendly Curmudgeons (Bob and Ray)

RAY: Ah, there's good news today, friends.
BOB: Good news for you, folks, bad news for us.
RAY: We've done it again, and our loss is your gain.
BOB: You see, in anticipation of the Easter season, we laid in a large supply of chocolate rabbits.

RAY: These were the best chocolate rabbits money could buy. Each one was genuine chocolate, all chocolate.

BOB: Each one had a purple ribbon tied around his or her neck.

RAY: Each one was edible, real edible.

BOB: But through the carelessness of one of our alert uniformed attendants, these chocolate rabbits were stored next to the steampipes, in our overstocked warehouse.

RAY: So, we are now able to offer, at a ridiculously low price, exactly twenty gross of genuine, laughably edible, all chocolate *wobblies.*

BOB: These wobblies are not only appropriate for any season, but the kiddies will have great fun trying to guess what the wobblies are supposed to represent. . . .

ANNOUNCER: Welcome to another episode of Wing Po—the true-to-life story of a Chinese philosopher who wanders across the American frontier in search of work. As our action-packed drama begins today, Wing Po has just entered the small, run-down saloon at Bitter Creek, and is approaching the bar.

BARTENDER: Howdy there, young fella. What'll it be?

PO: It will be as it has always been—for life is much like the rolling wheel of the oxcart. If we are to know how the spokes shall move on the next turn, we need only remember what they have done before.

BARTENDER: Oh. You're from out of town, ain't you?

BIFF: Hi, sports fans. This is Biff Burns and it's pregame dugout dialogue time. We're going to talk to the grizzled veteran of some twenty-odd years in baseball who today is finally retiring, Stuffy Hodgson. Stuffy, how do you feel?

STUFF: Well, I'm a bit sad, Biff. After all these years in the game . . . to realize this is my last day.

BIFF: That's a normal feeling to have, Stuff . . . but looking back, you've got to agree that the game's been pretty good to you.

STUFF: Not as good to me as it has been to some of these young punks coming along. . . . they have these radios, and they have all this music goin' in the locker room. I don't understand it. It's a bunch of noise. Whatever happened to Kate Smith . . . and Pat Boone . . . and them guys?

Bob Elliott (l.) and Ray Goulding (r.), the latter wearing a very heavy tie. Or is it Ray (l.) and Bob (r.)? (*Courtesy Bob and Ray*)

Whether satirizing baseball, David Carradine's TV series "Kung Fu," commercials, or their own ineptness, Bob Elliot and Ray Goulding are masters of understated comedy. Their background is in radio and their routines are, by necessity, verbally oriented. Even when they do a television show, they sit down to do their various bits. The cast of characters they have developed over their more than thirty years together is long. They have not changed their style since the forties, nor do they need to, and they pointed the way to future comedians and comedy teams. They were satirizing long before Nichols and May and Lenny Bruce, and they ad-libbed or wrote most of their material.

Robert Bracket Elliot was born in 1923 in Boston; Raymond Walter Goulding was born a year earlier in Lowell, Massachusetts. They were raised near Boston and both lost one or both of their parents when they were eighteen. Other than those facts there is no way to explain the uncanny way in which they can take almost any subject and ad-lib funny lines to each other. It is similar to the communication of Rowan and Martin, but Bob and Ray perfected it before Dan and Dick, and can do it with more polish and in various roles and guises.

Bob was an only child while Ray was one of four children. Ray's father worked in a textile mill and had the first radio in the neighborhood. With the help of his older brother, Phil, who was already an announcer, Ray began work at a local Lowell radio station when he was seventeen, making him one of the youngest announcers in radio. He had completed high school by this time and soon moved to a better job in Boston. After his tour in the army during World War II, he returned to Boston and joined station WHDH.

Bob grew up in a Boston suburb and used his high school PA system to put on radio shows; his roles ranged from Samuel Johnson to Sherlock Holmes. At seventeen, after finishing high school, he enrolled in a drama and radio school in New York, joining Angela Lansbury as an acting student. Like Jerry Lewis he was an usher (Radio City Music Hall) and later moved over to NBC as a page. Before he was twenty he had his first radio work on WINS in New York giving a "page boy's impressions of radio." He then moved closer to home and worked as an announcer at a Boston radio station until he joined the army in 1943.

In 1946 Bob was a disc jockey at WHDH in Boston and Ray gave the newscasts on Bob's show. Ray started lingering and malingering after his news broadcast and the two men exchanged lines and jokes between records. The team seemed a natural and listeners began haranguing the station

to hear more of their antics. "Matinee with Bob and Ray," their first show, was a half-hour spot that they were given in May 1946. That wasn't enough for their fans, so they were given an hour in the morning called "Break Fast with Bob and Ray."

They tried using scripts but quickly fell into the habit of just taking a premise and playing with it. Subsequent to their initial success, they began to build a stable of characters. Their first take-off on soap opera was "Linda Lovely." Their first character—aside from Bob and Ray ad-libbing— was Mary McGoon. They still use her thirty years later. Mary was joined by Wally Ballou, the bumbling reporter who always starts his interviews before he is on the air (". . .ly Ballou and today we're . . .") and has almost terminal adenoids. Some of the others to come along are Larry Lovebreath, Chester Hasbrouck Frisbie, and Wolfman, the worst person in the world.

They intermixed all the nonsense with a melange of sound effects: laughter, explosions, doors closing or opening or squeaking, footsteps, applause, Bronx cheers, breathing, rounds of drinking and eating, thunder, just about anything that did or did not apply to the situation. Ray has a deep baritone voice and a mastery of modulating the tones into various characters. He plays all the female characters and changes from decrepit old men to the guttural tones of Captain Wolf Larsen. Bob has a lighter baritone quality, almost lyric, and handles Akbar Mytai (a character from the soap spoof "Wayside Doctor"), who sounds like Peter Lorre, as well as foreign accents, droning monotones, and the pinched-nose twang of Ballou.

They continued building personalities and bits for five and a half years in Boston. In 1951 they lucked into an assignment in New York, replacing Ray's brother Phil and comedian Morey Amsterdam on a weekly show in New York. The show served as an audition and they got a contract with NBC to do a fifteen-minute show every night and an hour on Saturday. All of it was to be ad lib. They moved to New York and began doing their shows. They also added another daily show for two and half hours and fifteen minutes for NBC television in the evening. It was all live, before the days of tape, so if a breakdown came the network would cut to them and they started talking. This schedule got to them, as it would to any sane person, and they eventually decided to cut back their output.

But they had begun to lampoon everything: give-away shows, soap operas, and even commercials (they offered a ten-day course on how to become a ninety-seven-pound weakling, and sweaters in two different styles, turtle or V-neck. "State what kind of neck you have"). Naturally, sponsors did not take kindly to having their products treated in this satirical fashion. They moved from program to program and changed networks between 1952 and 1956. Due to their spoofs of products, they changed sponsors even more frequently. They had some difficulty adapting their verbal humor to television. After replacing Ray as the female in their bits on TV, Audrey Meadows later became Ralph Kramden's (Jackie Gleason) wife on the television series "The Honeymooners."

They had begun to do shows on tape and in 1956 they inaugurated their "critic-at-large" spots on NBC's "Monitor" radio show. These lasted for over eight years. Sometimes they did as many as fifteen spots on the Saturday and Sunday "Monitor" hours. In 1952 they received America's highest honor in radio, the Peabody Award, and again in 1957 for their shenanigans as entertainers and satirists.

Taking the battle with the sponsors one step farther, in '56 they started their own commercial company with ad man

Ed Graham and began doing commercials. They started with Piels beer and they stayed with the company until 1963. By 1970 they had done commercials for soups, banks, pliers, and peanut butter. In 1978 they are still seen doing American Express television commercials in their low-key, inimitable fashion. They were the pioneers in showing sponsors that approaching a product satirically could sell it. They also started an animated film company, doing take-offs on rotten films and classic books, but the overhead became too much. They did predate the animated cartoons that now inundate television on the weekends; they preceded "The Flintstones" which was the first big hit in the genre. In 1956 they made two albums, with other artists, for Coral Records: "Fun Time" and "Laugh of the Party."

In 1956 they were disc jockeys for Mutual (not one of the three major networks) and in '59 they did a daily radio show for CBS. They dropped out of radio in 1960 and just did commercials. In '62 they did a late afternoon show that lasted four hours and in '65 they again left radio. They started on TV and joined the "Today" show once a week in '66 and '67. Following "Today" they started making appearances on Johnny Carson's "Tonight" show and continue to do so in the late '70s.

They had been asked to do a show on Broadway but they were scared. They had never appeared before a live audience before and were concerned, too, about using the same material over and over; they were accustomed to ad-libbing. Finally they got over their qualms and in 1970 *Bob and Ray: The Two and Only* opened at the Golden Theatre, the same theater that had housed the successful Mike Nichols and Elaine May show in 1960. The critics were almost universal in their praise. The one holdout was New York critic John Simon. But as they handled the sponsors, Bob and Ray had the unique fun of getting back at their detractor in a later radio show. This dialogue ensued spontaneously

during "Mary Backstage, Noble Wife" (". . . the story of
America's favorite family of the footlights and of their fight
for security and happiness against the concrete heart of
Broadway").

CALVIN: Ah, who's the group of people in the back of the bus?
They keep passing around a paper bag and they all take a
swig out of it.

HARRY: I don't know. . . . They're having a good time, all right.

MARY: Well, they seem to be having more fun than we are, I'll
say that.

HARRY: Yes, and there across the aisle is John Simon. *(Loud
noise of crunching and chewing.)* He's got his lunch in a paper
bag. Look at the way he goes into a sandwich. Isn't that awful?

MARY: *(Shocked)* Right through the waxed paper and all.

HARRY: Must be hungry, I guess.

MARY: *(Crunching continues.)* He seems like he's always hungry.
I can't *bear* to watch him. I'm going to turn my back.

Back on Broadway at the Golden Theatre, all their nota-
ble characters were there among the overflowing props that
included hockey sticks, an old icebox, a pair of snowshoes, a
sewing machine, a large jar of marbles, and old radio mikes.
Bob and Ray came on stage and brought much of their
"family" with them: Wally Ballou, who had won "seventeen diction awards, two of which were cuff links . . .";
Leonard Bonfiglio, a checkout clerk who avoids checking out
"shepherd pies and canned Brunswick stew . . ."; the president of the "Slow Talkers of America"; Biff Burns and Stuffy
Hodgson; Larry Lovebreath; and many, many more.

The show ran on Broadway for six months and then
toured from Toronto to Fort Lauderdale, Florida. After the
live show they continued doing commercials and guest shots
on TV. In 1973 they were back to radio and continued their
same characters until 1976. They had made one film earlier,
but like most of the comedy teams after Dean and Jerry, it
was not a milestone in their career. They still do commercials

and have books on the stands with some of their best routines.

Bob and Ray have left a legacy of satire and have surely influenced a lot of the later teams. Their comical barbs at American institutions were never as politically direct as the Smothers Brothers, nor as sophisticated as Nichols and May. But they did do some political humor. As early as 1954 they had a character in "Mary Backstage, Noble Wife" (Commissioner Carstairs) who sounded suspiciously like Senator McCarthy (McCarthy was then indiscriminately trying to blacklist half of America as Communists). They did a take-off on then Vice–President Nixon's "Checkers" speech in the fifties and included him in their Broadway show in 1970. They did reports on the political conventions in 1968, too, but decided to stop that.

Radio had been weakening for a while when Bob and Ray started and they almost single-handedly helped revive the invalid for years. Their various absences from radio have been due to the sorry state of that medium. The uncanny ability they possess of seeming to know each other's mind is a marvel to behold. Even if they make a mistake it is incorporated into the routine they are doing. When they started in New York in 1952 they knocked out the leading radio comedy team, Rayburn and Finch.

Their characters were all distinct and fully realized and they existed as separate entities from the two comedians. This keynote establishes the trend after them. Dick Cavett, a man they parodied on Broadway, has said that they are "certainly as great as Nichols and May." If they didn't directly influence Mike and Elaine, they influenced them indirectly. It is impossible to end this section without using the oft-quoted tag lines of Bob and Ray:

This is Ray Goulding reminding you to write if you get work . . .
And Bob Elliot reminding you to hang by your thumbs.

They "Sang" Freud (Nichols and May)

Mike Nichols was not a member of the Actors Studio, which has produced such stars as Marlon Brando, Julie Harris, Ben Gazarra, Eva Marie Saint . . .
Miss May does not exist.

These wry liner notes from Nichols and May's first album in 1959 ("Improvisations to Music," Mercury Records) give some indication of their mutual passion for privacy and the lengths they went to protect it. They were the most hidden of the hidden comedians. Due to their propensity for saying outrageous things about themselves, it is difficult to establish what they actually were (and are) and what they actually did. Miss May told columnist Earl Wilson that her measurements were "24–35–127½." Mr. Nichols convinced many that he represented the United States on the Equestrian team in the 1958 Olympics. There was no mention of a horse.

Spawned by one of the early Chicago improvisation groups, the Compass Players (comedy team Stiller and Meara were members for a while), they developed, programmed, and epitomized the new form of comedy. They were the criterion to be judged by. They attacked their middle-class characters, the phony intellectuals, the would-be lovers, the machine-burdened city dweller, the psychiatrist's patient, from an actor's standpoint rather than a comedian's. They had the skill and timing to elicit laughs as they portrayed these modern antiheroes, but they seemed to do it as if oblivious to what was going on. At first happy with their success as performers, their quest for anonymity was one of the key reasons for the disbanding of the team after they had become heirs to the gap left by Martin and Lewis's schism in 1956. They separated less than six years after they banded together as a team and have almost desperately avoided the limelight ever since. Elaine May must be almost bound and gagged to be interviewed and except for a few stage appearances and three films, one of which she wrote and directed, she has given her time to writing and directing. Nichols, who assumes an even less distinct profile, turned entirely to directing for the stage and cinema.

Contrary to popular opinion, Elaine May does exist and Mike Nichols did study at the Actors Studio. Prior to that, Michael (Igor Peshkowsky) Nichols was born in Berlin in 1931. Getting no closer to Germany than her name, Elaine Berlin was born a year later in Philadelphia. Mike's father, an eminent physician, fled Nazi Germany. He brought his family to New York City, establishing a new practice and changing the family name to Nichols. Mike attended the best schools. He matriculated to the University of Chicago as a premed student. It was here that he first met Elaine Berlin and, according to her, they ". . . loathed each other at first sight."

While Mike was contending with the cultural change from Berlin to New York, Elaine was performing onstage and in radio with her father, Jack Berlin, an actor in the Yiddish theater. She did a Yiddish version of Baby Snooks on the radio called "Baby Noodnik." Instead of being shuttled off to relatives, like Joseph Levitch, Elaine traveled with the family and was constantly on the move. She got a respite from traveling in Los Angeles and began her schooling. She quit high school when she was fourteen and "sat around the house reading mostly fairy tales and mythology." She just did not like school. After three years of truancy and constant harassment by officials, she began sitting in on classes at the University of Chicago. She never bothered with formally enrolling but was in and about the school for several years. By this time she was Elaine May, not Elaine Berlin. How or why she trekked from Los Angeles to the University of Chicago is unknown. It is known that she was married and divorced as a teen-ager and, as a result, has a daughter and the last name of May.

Mike Nichols had forsaken medicine for acting. Whatever their real reactions after their first, brief meeting, Mike soon left college for acting and the actor's mecca, New York. He began studying with Lee Strasberg, known for his "method" theory of acting, at the Actors Studio. In a supple bit of one-upsmanship, Elaine had managed sometime before their reunion two years later to study with Marie Ouspenskaya, who was Lee Strasberg's teacher. From 1953 to 1955, while Mike was plying his craft in New York, Elaine was writing, acting, and directing in Chicago. Out of the campus Playwrights Theatre Club, the first improvisational group of any note, the Compass Players was born.

The "method" approach to acting involves many techniques to develop an actor's skills. One of these methods is improvisation: taking a character and a premise and developing them without the aid of a script or planning of any kind. The method was in fashion in the fifties so it was natural for people trained in this discipline to move on to a group that was purely improvisational. When performing improvs for an audience rather than as an exercise, comedy gets a quicker and a far better reaction. Hence, the various comedy improv groups of the '50s and '60s, most of them emanating from Chicago: the Compass Players, Second City, then the followers in the '70s, Ace Trucking Company, National Lampoon, and so on.

When Mike returned to Chicago he joined Elaine and the Compass Players, which had moved off-campus to a nightclub named The Compass. They remained there for three years, taking audience suggestions for characters and situations and then acting them out. They had not begun writing as a team yet, although Elaine had written on her own, but the very nature of improvisation gives rise to the actor being his own author.

The Compass troupe consisted of Elaine and Mike, comedian Shelley Berman, and three others. Later, Jerry Stiller and Anne Meara joined the group. Elaine had been taught the basics as a child onstage, and, like Bob and Ray, in radio. Mike now followed suit on a local Chicago radio station, introducing classical music as only a prep school DJ could and eventually being fired for yawning too much on an early morning program. He left the Compass to play an Italian immigrant on a Philadelphia (radio) soap opera called "Rittenhouse Square," which has all the earmarks of a Bob and Ray parody. Both Mike and Elaine held odd jobs during this period to pay the rent. Mike drove a post office truck and judged a jingle contest; Elaine was allegedly a private eye.

Mike left Philadelphia, Rittenhouse, and the Square, returning to improvs at the Compass. By now, Mike and Elaine were acutely aware of that strange affinity between them that characterizes all of the great comedy teams. When they did improvisations together things seemed to automatically fall into place. The Compass Players moved to St. Louis. There was an attempt to transplant the group to New York and, to that end, Mike and Elaine struck out for Manhattan in 1957 with approximately $39.50. They had toyed with the idea of breaking from the group and teaming. Stuck in New York with very little money, they hastily pursued the joint venture. They auditioned for manager Jack Rollins. He set them for an opening at the Blue Angel, which started many comedians to stardom, including Tom and Dick Smothers. The booking did not start for a week and, with their money shrinking, they urged Rollins to land them a gig at the Village Vanguard. They were readily accepted at both clubs and went on to play other night spots in New York and around the country.

Their stint in clubs perfected their style and the form that characterizes much of the later team comedy. In their albums and on Broadway most of their routines were set, even though written and developed by themselves through improvisation. In their formative years as a team they took the improv technique one step farther. The audience gave them suggestions, supplying an opening line, a closing line and a style or author. They wound up with suggestions that ranged from Aristotle to Dick Tracy. But they constantly proved they were the masters of the situation.

Their nightclub work led them to television. While at the Blue Angel, Jack Paar booked them on the original "Tonight" show, "The Jack Paar Show." Paar seemed to live at the Angel, grabbing the Smothers Brothers and countless others from the club. They did not go over well on Paar's show. They fared better on "The Steve Allen Show" and were undeniable hits on the January 1958 "Omnibus" show. They

Mike Nichols and Elaine May after seeing the King Tut exhibit. (circa 1960s) (*Courtesy Mike Nichols and Elaine May*)

were so good that their fee was up from under $300 a week in clubs to $5,000 an appearance on television. They guested on Dinah Shore's show and Perry Como's hour. They also did specials like "The Fabulous Fifties" in 1960. A year before that job they sold out New York's Town Hall in concert and, again, pointed the way toward the new wave: the move of comedians from the defunct nightclubs to concerts.

By this time they had made their first album, "Improvisations to Music," and it became a landmark as the first spoken comedy album to be a big seller. They were also in the vanguard of network vs. artist problems. Given their satirical approach, they ran into the same difficulties as Tom and Dick Smothers, only they did it seven years earlier. One of their "playlets" involved home permanents and intimated that sponsors controlled TV. As a result, they were "prevented" from appearing on the 1960 Emmy Awards. It is more than a coincidence that the sponsor for the Emmys manufactured home permanents. In 1967 Elaine joined the Smotherses on their show; her segment was cut out.

As late as 1965 Mike and Elaine followed Bob and Ray in doing guests shots on "Monitor" on radio and, also, in doing beer commercials. Earlier, in 1960, they paved the way (after composer-performers Comden and Green) for Bob and Ray's foray onto Broadway in 1970. First they tried the show on the road (à la the Marx Brothers), then they opened *An Evening with Mike Nichols and Elaine May* at the Golden Theatre in Shubert Alley on October 8, 1960. They wrote the material themselves, as they always had, but were aided by director Arthur Penn, who has since become a noted film director. They made an album of the show which was so popular it was reissued in '62 and '64. Their style and taste were evident. The liner notes were as always:

Mike Nichols is one of the most incisive wits in America today. His brilliance lights up the stage; his observations on the foibles of humanity rank with those of Jonathan Swift and George Bernard Shaw. He is without exception the world's greatest comedian.

Elaine May is a heck of a sweet kid.

The Broadway show consisted of more or less set routines and improvs, with the audience submitting premises. Southern playwright Alabama Gross (patterned after playwright Tennessee Williams) is effusively introduced by the dowdy PTA chairlady. Alabama allows as how the heroine of his new play is a woman who has "taken to drink, prostitution and puttin' on airs." A man in a phone booth desperately tries to explain to the stoic information operator ("Information, pleeeuuuuze") that his last dime has been lost, clinking into all of those other coins in the dime graveyard. He is late for a very important meeting and he agonizingly attempts to convince the implacable operator that she and her machine have taken his last dime. His helpless frustration finally wins him a supervisor who is worse than the original operator. After about ten minutes of pleading, he manages to get a sympathetic soul at the phone company; she puts his call through and he reaches: "This is a recording. You have dialed a wrong exchange."

A missile scientist at Cape Canaveral gets a call from his mother:

Melvin [Arthur on the album], this is your mother, do you remember me? . . . I don't want you to worry, Melvin, just because I had to go to the doctor again this week. Please don't worry. And don't think I don't understand why you don't call your poor sick mother. I do. I do understand, Melvin. You're too busy, that's all. Don't worry, Melvin, I understand. I understand. But I just want you to know, Melvin, that your poor sick mother is worried sick over you. I keep reading every day about all of those missiles of yours failing, and I'm worried sick that they'll take it out of your pay.

The show closed at the Golden in July 1961 and Elaine and Mike split up as a team. No explanation, no formal declaration was ever made. All that is known is that they occasionally did appear as a team for the next few years and that their parting was amicable. They reteamed at the inauguration of President Jimmy Carter but it is unlikely that anything more substantial than a rare benefit performance will be forthcoming.

Prior to *An Evening with*, Mike had struck out on his own, one venture on TV's "Playhouse 90," playing a role in the adaptation of the play *Journey to the Day*. After the break Elaine concentrated on her writing. Her play *Not Enough Hope* opened at the Maidman Theater in New York in February 1962. Another play by Elaine, *A Matter of Position*, reunited the two later in '62. It opened at the Walnut Street Theater in Philadelphia with Mike playing the role of Howard Miller. Neither play was a smash.

The duo continued to do sporadic television programs together and produced a third album, "Mike Nichols and Elaine May Examine Doctors" (Mercury, 1962). Both had separate careers now, he as a director, she as a writer, actress, director. The privacy they still strive for makes their break-up almost opaque. A sure way to achieve anonymity and remain in show business is to quit acting.

In 1963 Mike began his career as a director with the enormously successful Neil Simon comedy *Barefoot in the Park*. Things seemed to go easier for Mike than for Elaine. He received the Tony Award (Broadway's equivalent of Hollywood's Oscar) for directing *Barefoot*. He next directed Murray Schisgal's *Luv* and *The Knack* by British playwright Ann Jellicoe in 1964. He won another Tony and the New York Drama Critics Award for the production of *Luv*. In 1965 he returned to Neil Simon and won another Tony for directing *The Odd Couple*. While branching out into films in 1966, he maintained his involvement with Broadway through the late '70s: *The Apple Tree* with Julie Harris ('66), a revival of Lillian Hellman's *The Little Foxes* ('67), Simon's *Plaza Suite* ('68), a revival of Noel Coward's *Design for Living* at L.A.'s Ahmanson Theater ('70), Simon's *Prisoner of Second Avenue* with Peter Falk ('71), Chekhov's *Uncle Vanya* with Nicol Williamson, Julie Christie, and George C. Scott ('73), David Rabe's controversial *Streamers* at the Long Wharf Theater and later at Lincoln Center in New York ('75), and a British play, *Comedians,* at the Music Box Theater in New York ('76). In 1977 he directed *The Gin Game* on Broadway, starring Hume Cronyn and Jessica Tandy.

Having no film experience, Mike was given the formidable task of directing Edward Albee's award-winning play *Who's Afraid of Virginia Woolf* in its screen adaptation. The cast consisted of Richard Burton, Elizabeth Taylor and the relatively new Sandy Dennis and George Segal. This time he won the National Association of [Movie] Theater Owners award for Director of the Year. He moved on to *The Graduate* in 1967 with stars Dustin Hoffman and Anne Bancroft. He won an Oscar for that effort. His other films include *Catch-22* ('70) from Joseph Heller's novel, *Carnal Knowledge* ('71), *Day of the Dolphin* with George C. Scott ('73), and *The Fortune* ('74). Even though the last two or three were not financial successes, Mike Nichols is considered one of the best film and stage directors in the world. He is one of the few film directors that get "final cut," which means that no studio executive comes in and botches up his work.

He did not neglect TV entirely. In the mid-sixties "The Many Worlds of Mike Nichols" was an ABC special, starring Julie Andrews, Eli Wallach, Richard Burton, Walter Matthau, Elizabeth Taylor, and . . . Elaine May. The special was written by Buck Henry, who wrote the screenplays of *Catch-22* and *Day of the Dolphin* and created the TV series "Get Smart" with Mel Brooks. In the mid-seventies Mike co-wrote "Julie and Carol at Carnegie Hall" with Ken Welch. The special starred Carol Burnett and Julie Andrews and Mike added an Emmy to his list of awards. In 1976–77 he was executive producer of ABC's TV series "Family." Sometime during his crowded schedule he accepted an honorary doctorate in humane letters from the University of Rochester in New York.

Elaine was active but did not emerge as a full talent until almost ten years after the split. And that took a great deal of doing. She had her share of problems with the networks; next she took on the studios. In 1964 Elaine directed a play Off-Broadway in New York (*The Third Ear*). The next year she acted in her first film, *Enter Laughing*, Carl Reiner's adaptation of his play. In '66 she made her second film, *Luv*, and returned to stage acting at the Henry Miller Theater in *The Office*. In 1965 there was a fourth Nichols and May album, "The Best of Nichols and May," but it relied on previously recorded material. She wrote and directed her one-act play *Adaptation* for the off-Broadway Greenwich Mews Theater in 1969. She also directed the second one-act on the bill, Terence McNally's *Next*, and continued directing chores for three tours of the plays.

In 1971 Elaine accomplished an unusual feat: she wrote, directed, and co-starred with Walter Matthau and James Coco in the film, *A New Leaf*. But she did not have "final cut." The arguments between her and Paramount escalated until she sued to keep the film from opening. The hassles, lawsuits, extended budget, and the three years it took to make the film were not assuaged by the movie opening and doing little business.

In 1972 she moved to another studio and directed *The Heartbreak Kid;* her daughter, actress Jeannie Berliner, co-starred in the comedy-romance. This was not a financial winner either. In early '73 she somehow wound up back with Paramount to direct her own script *Mikey and Nicky,* starring Peter Falk and John Cassavettes. It took more than three years and three times as much film as *Gone With the Wind* to get the film released. The lawsuits alone will probably drag into the eighties.

Mikey and Nicky was not well received by the critics, or the public. The film is in the ultrarealistic style of the early Cassavettes' films and the much earlier neorealism of post-World War II Italian films. The plot is simply one night in the lives of two small-time hoods; they grew up as boyhood friends and now one is compelled to "finger" the other for a gangland killing. The latest studio wrangle was May's rewrite of an earlier film, *Here Comes Mr. Jordan.* Paramount did not allow May to direct the film and replaced her with Warren Beatty ("Shampoo") and Buck Henry. The film was released under the title of *Heaven Can Wait.*

Sangfroid is a French term that means coolness of mind, composure. As a team, Nichols and May had sangfroid. Mike still seems to have it. The two confronted the audience in a battle of wits and always emerged victorious. They took team comedy out of straight lines and jokes and into characters and situations. The only team to deal with the psychological aspects of their characters before Nichols and May were Bob and Ray. And the latter team did not push and delve as deeply. Many of Mike and Elaine's routines revolve around the psychiatrist-patient relationship. In their album on doctors, "Transference" has a woman psychiatrist mothering her patient as he tries to figure out why he sees her as a mother figure. In "Merry Christmas, Doctor" a patient (Mike) explains that he cannot make his usual session on Friday, Christmas Eve. His shrink (Elaine) becomes upset. (She: "I'm not upset." He: "I'll be back on Monday. You know that." She begins to have a nervous breakdown. "I'm not hurt. I'm going to analyze it." He: "It's very simple. I'd

rather be with my wife and children than you on Friday."
She: "Oh . . ." She becomes hysterical and shouts, "Get out!
Get out! Get out!")

In this way Mike and Elaine laid bare the underlying
frailties of all of us while making us giddy with laughter.
They also satirized our values from quiz shows to then
President Dwight Eisenhower and the U-2 spy plane inci-
dent.

The improvised style is not new. In Renaissance Italy the
commedia dell'arte followed a similar form, stock characters
improvised various *lazzi* or jokes. They had several basic
plots but varied the sections between beginning and end.
The improv groups revived the form but it took Nichols and
May to perfect it and to present it to a wide audience. In
this alone, they were unique. It also led to their being one of
the first teams to write their own material exclusively. The
trend that was started in the thirties—having someone else
write your material—had been in force generally until Bob
and Ray and then Mike and Elaine changed the system.
The trend toward writers had begun in radio; Fibber McGee
and Molly were singers, not comedians, and started their
radio hit with a scripted show. Film also necessitated the
use of writers so even the ad-lib nonsense of the Marx four
became a scenario, however loose.

The subtlety of Mike and Elaine's humor was also a new
element. Bob and Ray were considered to be too subtle for
some and lost one show as a result. Nichols and May were
even more subtle, but as the number of college-educated,
World War II offspring began to mature, there was a larger
audience that would laugh at their humor. This boundary-
breaking team also made the first financial breakthrough in
albums, the first American comedy team Broadway success,
and was one of the earliest to do comedy concerts. If they
were not as well known as the other two blockbuster teams
of the sixties, Rowan and Martin and the Smothers Broth-

ers, it is because they were subtler, never exposed regularly on TV (indeed it is a medium that, like the Smothers, they would have had difficulty in), and they broke up after five or six years.

Nichols and May could create real, funny people by just talking or perhaps using one or two props, like a phone. The last times they did that were 1972 at Madison Square Garden in New York for a benefit involving George McGovern's presidential campaign and in '76 for Carter's inauguration. Most likely they will never retrace those steps, so if you find a Nichols and May album hang onto it. It's funny and it's worth a lot of money.

Hershey Horowitz Marries Mary Elizabeth Doyle and Lives Happily Ever After (Stiller and Meara)

Hershey (Hesh) Horowitz is a Jewish bagel baker from East Forty-second Street in Flatbush, New York. Mary Elizabeth Doyle is a Catholic girl who lives on the same block. Even though they grew up on the same street, they have no mutual friends and are burdened with conflicting religious, social, and eating habits. A computer with questionable taste has matched them up for a date. With all of their differences, they can't seem to find a basis for a relationship of any kind. But they decide that their differences really don't matter. They like each other and that is all that's important. It's Friday so Mary can't have meat; they compromise by going to Ratner's delicatessen for some "filtered fish." ("That's gefilte fish.")

Thus runs the scenario for Stiller and Meara's best-known routine, "Hershey Horowitz Meets Mary Elizabeth Doyle." The progression here is an unusual one for sketch comedy. Unlike a two- or three-act play, a film, or the continuing characters on a TV series, characters in a sketch are almost always caricatures lacking in dimension. They must be immediately identifiable, have an obvious problem, and then in six, eight, or ten minutes they must attempt to resolve the problem. As acting and improvisation began taking over the style of comedy teams, Stiller and Meara progressed from a satirically resolved situation to a dramatically resolved one. They added drama to satire.

Mike Nichols and Elaine May, as boss and shy secretary, go to a bar; he bumblingly attempts to get her to his apartment to listen to a new Kostelanetz record. The humor is in his fumbling and her embarrassment. She acquiesces and they leave. Hershey and Mary Elizabeth do not conquer their differences and should probably just decide that the computer made a mistake. Instead, they say goodbye, then stop because they realize that their caring about each other is more important than religious and social differences. The satire of those differences gives way to the drama of their emotions.

Jerry Stiller is Jewish and Anne Meara *was* Catholic—she converted to Judaism when their first child was born in 1962. It would seem pertinent to say that the new style of comedy, the differing religious and social backgrounds, and marriage seem to have guided Stiller and Meara to a depth beyond just satire. It might even explain their longevity as a team, given these swift, modern times. But, it is rough to make any sense of these religious-social couplings. Whatever the judgment, Stiller and Meara are funny.

Gerald Stiller was born in New York in 1928 and was raised in Brooklyn. His father, a bus driver, wanted him to be a dental technician, but Jerry wanted to run around the streets with the three other kids in the family. Anne Meara was christened in 1933 and grew up in a Jewish neighborhood on Long Island. She wanted to be a Shakespearean actress, which may not have appealed to her father, the lawyer.

Anne finished high school and became an apprentice in

stock. Stock is summer theater that consists of plays that make one-week stops in different towns for six or more weeks. Each theater carries its own apprentices who mainly work very hard as gofers: moving sets, getting props, and, on rare occasions, getting to perform one or two lines. After running up and down aisles a lot, Anne moved on to New York City and studied with Uta Hagen at the HB (Herbert Berghof) Studios, an acting school that is ranked highly along with the Actors Studio. She began getting stage roles and played with Zero Mostel in *Ulysses in Nighttown* and with Michael Redgrave in *A Month in the Country*. She was soon doing small roles on television.

Jerry came out of the army and studied acting at Syracuse University. He did stock in the summer and finally left for the real world, appearing in the national company of *Peter Pan* and doing roles from Shakespeare to revues in numerous places like the Phoenix Theatre in New York, the Shakespeare Festival at Stratford, Connecticut, and Billy Barnes's Showboat in Chicago.

In New York actors make the rounds, which means that they go to agents' offices and out on auditions almost daily. It's a large city but the acting community is not very large, so it is not astounding that Jerry and Anne met after a while. As a matter of fact, they met at an agent's office. It was 1954 and two months later they were married.

There was no thought of being a comedy team but they wanted to be together. They joined Joseph Papp's Shakespeare in the Park in its early days. Jerry did character roles and Anne played leading ladies. They were married, they were happy, they were working together. However, they wanted to have a family and they could not do it on their salaries.

They considered the possibilities and came up with the idea for a comedy team. They were both funny and they were quite different. In their own way, each had a distinctive physical and mental outlook that could make them a male and female Laurel and Hardy. Jerry is shorter than Anne who is a statuesque redhead. In 1962 Stiller and Meara became a team. They tried small clubs and found themselves with the Compass Players. They went on to

Jerry Stiller and Anne Meara. (*Courtesy Stiller and Meara*)

two revues in Chicago, *Happy Medium* and, in the "son of" tradition, *Medium Rare,* which ran for two years. They played London (*The Establishment*) and New York clubs like the Village Gate and the ever-popular Blue Angel.

Would-be talk-show hosts had talent coordinators scouring places like the Blue Angel, for new comedians and comedy teams. Jerry and Anne did Merv Griffin's talent showcase and this led to a guest spot on Ed Sullivan's Sunday night variety hour. Sullivan signed them to a six-shows-a-year contract and they made more than thirty appearances on the show. Their first album, "The Last Two People on Earth," was released in 1967 and they began playing bigger clubs, reaching Las Vegas. They also continued to do other TV shows, specials, and summer stock.

Perhaps because their comedy was similar to Nichols and May, what the press labeled "anxiety comedy," or perhaps because they took that step further in drama, they were successful but did not become major stars. They also had to contend with the overwhelming popularity of the Smothers Brothers and Rowan and Martin, both of whom had become starring teams when Stiller and Meara started their climb. They didn't like clubs any longer and wanted to stay close to their family; they had two children now and did not want to run all over the country.

They took Bob and Ray's cue and did commercials. In 1969 they signed with Blue Nun wine and have been doing comedy spots for them ever since. Their last contract was for three years at $300,000. He: "I noticed a little blue nun next to the fruit compote." She: "It's probably Teresa Pensibini. We always knew she had the calling." Despite this success, in 1970 they decided to pursue separate careers, occasionally getting together for Blue Nun and other commercials, ranging from Jack-in-the-Box restaurants to dictating equipment, and a stage turn in stock. In '71 they made their second album "Laugh When You Like."

Anne did two movies, Neil Simon's *The Out-of-Towners* with Jack Lemmon, and *Lovers and Other Strangers*. She was a regular in an ABC summer replacement series "The Corner Bar." Jerry was an associate producer on that series but he was not doing as well as Anne. He did stock and some TV game shows, but his career alone was not skyrocketing. Even with their extensive acting background, Jerry and Anne were known as comedians. It was hard to convince people that they had been actors before they became comedians. Eventually, they both did.

In 1974 Anne did a lead in a television show, "Medical Center," and that resulted in her getting an Emmy nomination in her own series "Kate McShane" in 1975. The character of Kate was a hard-boiled lawyer. From there she became Sally, Valerie Harper's friend, on "Rhoda" and was nominated for another Emmy in 1976.

Jerry began surfacing in films like *Airport 1975* and *The Taking of Pelham One Two Three*. In '75 he got a series, "Joe and Sons." Neither that series nor "Kate McShane" ran for very long. Jerry then starred on Broadway and in the film version of *The Ritz*, playing an inept lower-echelon Mafia type in the comedy. He and Anne were reunited in the film *Nasty Habits*, Jerry doing a cameo.

Now that they have both established separate careers, they enjoy working together all that much more. They are in the process of doing a new mini-mini-series called "Take 5." The spots are five-minute sketches, 175 of them, that play at varying times on TV. An improvisational ninety-second radio series of a similar nature has been started locally in Los Angeles by the team of Alan Barzman and Pat McCormick. McCormick is a comedian and writer on the Johnny Carson show and plays a Jonathan Winters–Mel Brooks series of impromptu characters to Barzman's straight man. Stiller and Meara crop up individually and together on game shows like

"Tattletales" and "The $25,000 Pyramid" and they also do guest appearances and specials.

Stiller and Meara's comedy is in the mold of the sixties. They are bright and their characters have an added depth as opposed to many of Nichols and May's portrayals. Jerry and Anne do not match Mike and Elaine's sophistication and their satire is not as biting. As most teams of the period, they write most of their own material but they do not write all of their commercial copy. They grew out of improvisation and acting schools but they are less hidden than Mike and Elaine because there is more of Anne and Jerry in many of their characters.

Machines have always given people problems in comedies. Laurel and Hardy had a near world war with automobiles. The improvs utilized the phone a great deal and, hence, comedian Shelley Berman was known for his phone bits, as were Nichols and May. Stiller and Meara use the phone, too,

Stiller and Meara in a scene from their new syndicated TV show, "Take 5." (*Courtesy Stiller and Meara*)

but update the usage by calling into a radio or TV show or getting fouled up with computer dating.

As a team they are even more evident than Rowan and Martin presently are. But the situation is not the same for either team as it was when Martin and Lewis or Nichols and May were at the top. For Anne and Jerry, their marriage is sound, given the ballast of their independent careers, and their team will probably remain sound. Like the only other married comedy teams, Burns and Allen and Fibber McGee and Molly, they settled into one team and that was enough.

The Tall Bald Man with One Short Jew (Reiner and Brooks)

Carl Reiner is a tall, bald, Jewish man and Mel Brooks is a short Jewish man. Unlike Elaine May, they do not exist; at least not as a team. They don't play clubs or concerts and they have never made a film or a TV series. They are unique in being the only closet comedy team in the world. They came out of the closet long enough to make four albums from 1960 to 1973 and, on that basis, they have a large cult of fans who hunger for the terse, basic philosophy of the 2,000-year-old man.

The 2,000-year-old man (Mel Brooks) is a wizened Jewish man who has lived for 2,000 years and has opinions about everything. He has been married many times ("400, 500 wives, countless, countless wives"), and has had 42,000 children ("And not one comes to see me!"). His progeny number 21,000 doctors, 700 accountants, and 2 entertainers.

CARL: What was your diet like 2,000 years ago?

MEL: 2,000 years ago we only ate what God meant, the organic and natural.

CARL: Like what?

MEL: Clouds, stars, rocks. . . . Did you know that many parts of a pine tree are edible? . . . Pussy willows make a lovely dessert.

CARL: . . . Did you believe in any superior being?

MEL: Yeh, a guy Phil . . . we prayed to him.

CARL: . . . How long was his reign?

MEL: Not too long. One day Philip was hit by lightning and we looked up and said, "There's something bigger than Phiiiiiiilllll!

CARL: . . . How did the word shower come to be?

MEL: Most words come from onomatopoeia.

CARL: You mean they sound like what they are . . .

MEL: You go in a shower you get sssssssshhhhhhhh.

CARL: But that's not shower, that's . . .

MEL: But when they added hot water . . . then you walked in and you said, "OOOOWWWW!" Ssssssshhhhhhooooooowwwwwer.

CARL: . . . Why do you call a nose a nose?

MEL: What are you gonna blow, your eyes?

In the mid-twenties, somewhere in Brooklyn, Melvyn Kaminsky was born. In the Bronx, New York, in 1922, Carl Reiner played straight man to his mother and was born. Melvyn became funny at an early age through need; he was short and wanted to survive the wrath of the bigger guys on the block so he made them laugh any way he could. He learned the drums and longed to be a pilot or a chemist. Since he couldn't fly and he had trouble with addition, he played the skins after school and during summer vacation. He finished a year of college and got drummed into the army.

Carl went from high school to being a shipping clerk, then a machinist's helper. He joined a drama school and then a little theater. He next played in summer stock and worked on the Borscht circuit. In the army his first sergeant was Howard Morris, another comedian (now a director) whom he later worked with in television. In 1946 Carl left the service and decided that comedy, not acting, would be his pursuit. He worked in and around New York City, opening in a revue, *Inside U.S.A.*, on Broadway in '48. *Alive and Kicking*, his next show on the Great White Way, exposed him to producer Max Liebman. Liebman signed him to emcee and do character roles on NBC's "Your Show of Shows," starring comic Sid Caesar. Howard Morris was also a character comedian on the show. "Your Show of Shows" was rivaled only by Milton Berle and "I Love Lucy" as the top comedy shows of the early and mid-fifties.

Visualizing the 2,000-year-old man deactivating land mines during the Battle of the Bulge in 1944 is a little hard. The 2,000-year-old man, as everyone knows, hates wars except for one.

MEL: There was one good war. The War of the Roses was a just war.
CARL: Why was it just?
MEL: We went to sleep Wednesday night and when we woke up Thursday there wasn't a rose in the whole country.

But there Mel was in the middle of one of the largest battles of World War II. Melvyn was honorably discharged and continued playing drums in the Catskill Mountains, the home of the Borscht Belt. He changed his name to avoid confusion with trumpet player Max Kaminsky. As Mel Brooks he did summer stock, some radio, and wound up as social director at Grossinger's, one of the largest hotels in the Catskills. He also played drums with a saxophonist named Sid Caesar. Caesar was breaking in as a comedian and asked Mel to write some comedy material for "Broadway Revue," an NBC television series. When Sid starred in "Your Show of Shows" in 1950, Mel was one of the writers, although he had to work his way up.

Carl and Mel met on "Shows," their jobs overlapping: Mel sometimes did a role on the show, Carl sat in on many of the writers' conferences. "Your Show of Shows" ran for four

Mel Brooks (l., without his 2,000-year-old man cape) and Carl Reiner (r.) with his 2,000-year-old toupee (late 1970s). (*Courtesy Warner Bros. Records*)

years and then gave way to "Caesar's Hour," which was succeeded by "Sid Caesar Invites You" in 1957. Carl and Mel stayed with all three shows, but when the last series failed in 1958 they were both unemployed. Carl was the best "second banana" on TV and had no trouble landing roles in films and multiple television shows. Mel, who had no qualifications except being insanely funny and telling jokes on top of coffee tables while imitating Al Jolson and tap dancing, was out of work for a year and a half.

Carl expanded his acting to include writing, first scripting Dinah Shore's variety show and then publishing his first novel, *Enter Laughing* in 1958. The book was later done on Broadway and made into a film in which Elaine May made her cinematic debut as an actress (1965). Sometime during their "Your Show of Shows" days Mel and Carl began doing impromptu comedy bits for friends. They were all ad lib with Carl asking outrageous questions and Mel being more outrageous as an "astronaught" or a Tibetan monk.

But the character that everyone loved was the 2,000-year-old man. Friends always requested the bit at parties and Steve Allen convinced Mel and Carl to make an album.

Hot on the grooves of Nichols and May's success with their first album, in 1960–61 "2,000 Years with Carl Reiner and Mel Brooks" came out on the Capitol label. The album was an instant success and prompted "2,001 Years with Reiner and Brooks" in 1962 and "Reiner and Brooks at the Cannes Film Festival" in 1963.

Things were going so well they even tried a variation on the 2,000 year old man, doing an interview with the two-hour-old baby. The baby was funny but not as funny as the talkative old man. When the albums went out of circulation there was such a demand for a fourth album, "2,000 and Thirteen: Carl Reiner and Mel Brooks," was cut in 1973. They still avoided clubs for the most part and only occasionally showed up on television, usually on a talk show. Carl would wear a tie and present the sane, logical world. Carl is an excellent straight man and kept Mel from going bananas. Mel wore a long black cape and a black fedora as the 2,000-year-old man. When asked about his knowledge of Jesus he responded:

MEL: I knew him. Nice boy. He wore sandals. He was quiet, a quiet lad. He came into the store, never bought anything. . . . He made a cabinet for me.
CARL: Did you know he was going to be the Jesus that shook the world?
MEL: If I knew that he was going to be a hit I would have made him a partner in the store.

The first album meant a change for Mel Brooks. He had written a few specials for stars like Victor Borge and Andy Williams, but now he was becoming known as a completely

lovable wacko. By 1965 the first albums had sold over two
million copies and led Mel the way of Bob and Ray, Nichols
and May, and Stiller and Meara: he did beer commercials
for Ballantine. Earlier he had written some Broadway shows
—*New Faces of 1952*, a revue; *Shinbone Alley*, a musical
in 1957, and *All American*, another musical in 1962. None
of them were overwhelming hits. His real success, after "Your
Show of Shows" and the 2,000-year-old man, was to be in
films. He wrote a trailer for a film that was better than the
film and then made a short that he conceived, wrote, and
narrated, *The Critic*. That earned him an Oscar for best
short subject (1963).

Following that he went on to create the spy spoof TV
series "Get Smart" with Buck Henry. The show ran from
1965 to 1970. He officially launched his movie career with
The Producers which he wrote and directed in 1968. That
won him an Academy Award for best original screenplay.
He went on to write, direct, and act in a series of comedy
films that keeps him ranked with Woody Allen in first place
as the two funniest filmmakers in Hollywood: *The Twelve
Chairs* ('70), *Blazing Saddles* ('74), *Young Frankenstein*
('75), *Silent Movie* ('76) and *High Anxiety* ('77). He was
involved in another TV series in the mid-'70s, a satire on
Robin Hood, but not getting a favorable reaction and disliking the present TV series format, he bowed out and the
show went off the air.

Carl Reiner never had the slump that Mel did. His writing
and acting carried him through until he originated, produced, and acted in "The Dick Van Dyke Show" in 1961.
That series won eleven Emmys in its long run and is still
airing in syndication in the late seventies. Carl produced
and/or wrote and/or directed a number of film projects
(*Enter Laughing*) and television shows ("The New Dick
Van Dyke Show"). His most recent movie, which he di-

rected and co-write is *Oh, God* (1977). It stars singer John Denver and former comedy team member George Burns. After the financial success of this picture, Carl has more films planned. He has also produced a son, Rob Reiner, who has been Michael Stivic, Archie's son-in-law, on Norman Lear's popular sitcom "All In The Family" since the show's inception.

Carl and Mel are friends and see each other frequently but they have no interest in playing Vegas as a duo. All of their album material was improvised—Carl asking, Mel blurting out whatever occurred to him. They are both writers and simply write with their minds and tongues as they improvise their routines. Mel plays the same character. Unlike the norm for other teams of the sixties and seventies, they do not act out scenes. Mel harks back to a burlesque-vaudeville style that is also different than the more cerebral sketches of the last two decades. Without marijuana and ethnic references, his humor is much like Cheech and Chong. There is satire in the 2,000-year-old man but it is not the pointed conviction that spurred Nichols and May and, even further, the Smothers Brothers. Asked what to do about America's economic problems, the 2,000-year-old man answers simply:

MEL: Sell America.
CARL: To who?
MEL: Japan. They're going to get it in ten years anyway.

The real intent is laughter; thought is only an afterthought. Paul Revere is referred to as anti-Semitic:

MEL: They're coming! They're coming! The Yiddish are coming!
CARL: He said the British are coming.
MEL: OY! I'll have to write his wife a note. I didn't even go to the funeral.

CARL: What is the greatest medical discovery in 2,000 years? Transplants? Antibiotics? The heart-lung machine?

MEL: Liquid Prell.

CARL: You equate Liquid Prell with the heart-lung machine?

MEL: Wait a minute. Your heart-lung machine is in your medicine cabinet and falls out, it's gonna break.

When Mel went on Johnny Carson's show alone, the bit did not go as well. The chemistry that Carl and Mel have is, as with all good teams, not that easy to come by. Carl and Mel make people laugh through their many separate projects, but to some of us they will always be known as Reiner and Brooks, the closet comedy team.

Man and Machine (Burns and Schreiber)

JACK BURNS: Even when Avery and I were playing Vegas, we were actors pretending to be stand-up comics.

The comedy team of Jack Burns and Avery Schreiber exemplified many of the elements dominant in the last two decades. Jack was a radio man and both men were members of an improv company. They played characters in sketches, not themselves telling jokes. Avery is Jewish, Jack is Catholic. Their routines were set but they developed them through improvisation and wrote the material themselves. They took Stiller and Meara's move to drama in their playlets to a more subtle study of loneliness and alienation. The lack of communication between the two characters in Jack and Avery's best-known piece ("The Cab Driver") is the basis of the routine's humor as well as the keynote to their style. They finally arrived at the furthest poles of modern man's attempt to reach someone other than himself in a sketch that has Avery portraying a very human-like machine that offers the only solace that Jack, a lonely, drunk, loser can find.

John Francis Burns was born in Boston in 1933. Like the Smothers Brothers, he was the son of a military man. In 1951, after high school, he entered the Marines and then studied at the Leland Powers radio school in Boston while working part-time at a local radio station. By 1956 Jack seemed to be taking a straight newsman's course. He became news director of an NBC radio affiliate in Boston, even going to Cuba to do one of the last interviews with Fidel Castro. Comedian George Carlin was then a DJ at the same station and they met and started doing comedy on the air together in 1959. Whether the NBC affiliate was approving or not, they promptly moved on to a radio show in Fort Worth, Texas. Texas was not their best state. They played a club in Dallas and were promptly arrested.

The act really wasn't that bad. They had just arrived in Dallas and they took some things to the cleaners. George happened to have a news clipping in one of the shirts to be cleaned and on the opposite side of the clipping there was a story about two men holding up an automobile club. George returned for the clothes the next day and a mini-army of plainclothes policemen jumped from behind counters, hang-- ers, and irons and arrested him. They also rounded up Jack.

Jack and George decided that there were better places to be improperly arrested. In 1960 they moved to Los Angeles. This time the police left them alone but their apartment was robbed a few days after they arrived. They showed up for an audition at L.A. radio station KDAY with a lot less than Nichols and May had when the latter moved to New York (about $1.50). But they got the job. They also started doing their act at a local coffeehouse, Cosmo's Alley. Coffeehouses were the standard showcases for comics in the late fifties and early sixties. Comic Lenny Bruce caught their act at Cosmo's and helped them get an agent and a stint at the Cloisters in Chicago. After one month in L.A. they had a morning radio show, a regular night gig, and then a job on the road.

The team stayed together for two years and then decided to break up. Their material was considered hip, at least hip enough for the rule-breaking Lenny Bruce, but even though satirical, they did not do the shock humor that Bruce was known for. They did characters and, having a similar background (Irish–Catholic), the characters tended to be similar. That can wear out fairly quickly. They were too close in spirit, appearance, and comedic style to make a workable team. Comedy teams are composed of opposites, usually physically and temperamentally. Except for married teams, most comedy teams do not even socialize very often when not working. Even Bob and Ray, the longest existing team that is working, or Rowan and Martin, who have been together for twenty-five years, do not see each other often in a social context. But Burns and Carlin played clubs for two years and made one album, "Burns and Carlin at the Playboy Club," which sold about thirty copies until George Carlin became a comedy superstar in the seventies. The album was reissued and Jack still gets residual checks. After the act broke up in 1962, Jack gravitated to Chicago and the Second City, the best-known of all the improv groups and the most important one after the Compass Players.

Avery Schreiber first saw light in 1935 and there is a rumor that even then he had a large bushy mustache that looked like two of the world's largest, hairiest caterpillars fighting over somebody's mouth. Avery finished school and went to the Goodman Theater of the Art Institute of Chicago, one of the more respected dramatic schools in the country. He studied acting and improvisation under noted improv master Viola Spolin. He performed his army years and then became involved, quite logically, in the Second City in 1960. Two years later Jack and Avery met, and they soon began finding that untaught timing that makes comedy teams. Their different backgrounds and differing looks added up to an eventual teaming—Jack is tall, fair and conspicuously Irish; Avery is chubby and has dark curly hair and the caterpillar mustache. When the Second City was performing at Square East in New York's Greenwich Village in 1964, a bizarre thing happened. Someone from the Jack Paar show had taken a wrong subway train and, instead of winding up at the Blue Angel, saw Jack and Avery do their cab-driver routine. That led to their first TV appearance on Paar's show and they were formally a team.

"The Cab Driver" is a study in opposites. A street-wise New York Jewish cabbie picks up a fare. The patron is a small-town, Archie Bunker type. This guy doesn't think of himself as a bigot but as a man of the world, knowing how to solve the world's problems and intent on doing just that.

CABBIE *(Schreiber)*: Where to, friend?

CONVENTIONEER *(Burns)*: Right to the Hotel Astor. Room 518.

CABBIE: They stop me on the fourth floor.

CONVENTIONEER: I got ya', I got ya', I got ya' . . . Yeah, Yeah! We're havin' fun here. Y'see we're here at a convention. Everyone's here from the home office. The whole gang's here. "Hail, hail the gang's . . ." They're all here. I'll tell ya' who's here: Danny Cronin, Tommy Johnson, Eddie Nolan. Patrick L. Bright's here, Jimmy Noonan . . .

CABBIE: I don't know any of those guys, y'know? . . . You're alone back there, right?

CONVENTIONEER: Yeh . . . sure.

CABBIE: Just checking. You know.

CONVENTIONEER: . . . You know what I hate?

CABBIE: I've got a good idea.

CONVENTIONEER: . . . I hate those people who make derogatory remarks about someone's ancestry. You've heard it, you've heard it! . . . You know who says that the most?

CABBIE: Who's that?

CONVENTIONEER: Your Hunkies. A'right, we're having fun here, we're having fun here! All the guys brought their wives. I was gonna bring my wife but we've been separated twelve years.

CABBIE: Good idea not to bring her.

CONVENTIONEER: Oh, yeh. You kidding me? She was a *saint!* She was too good for me. I was a bum, she's a saint. She's a saint. Here I got a picture of her right here. That's a saint! That's a saint!

CABBIE: Yeah, I never saw one before.

CONVENTIONEER: Of course not, you're Jewish. You don't have saints.

CABBIE: We got prophets . . .

Burns and Schreiber got national attention through numerous TV shots. They played better clubs, and in 1967 their first album, "In One Head and Out the Other," came out. But they broke up the same year. The reasons are vague but it came down to a need to make it individually on their own—just as Stiller and Meara needed to do the same thing three years later. Jack returned to L.A. and did television, soon replacing Don Knotts on "The Andy Griffith Show." As most of the sixties teams had done, they wrote their own act, and Jack started writing on his own during the separation. Avery went to San Francisco and acted and directed the Committee, another improv group that was an offshoot of the Second City. He went on to give an award-winning performance in the Story Theater production of "Metamorphoses" and co-starred in the ill-fated series "My Mother the Car." He wrote, too, and was one of the scripters of "Zero Hour," a TV special starring Zero Mostel. Avery also started his extensive commercial repertoire. He is particularly identified as the "cruncher" for Dorito corn chips.

In 1972 Jack and Avery chose to team again. They got together by accident while doing a benefit for a school in

Los Angeles that Schreiber's children attended. They started doing TV spots on Johnny Carson's show and bigger clubs in Tahoe and Vegas. In 1973 they recorded their second album, "Pure B.S.," and an ABC special. The network almost didn't put the special on, thinking it was not geared to the mass audience. But the network was wrong. The show was a hit and led to a summer replacement series that same year entitled "The Burns and Schreiber Comedy Hour."

The show was comprised of sketches with Jack playing his conventioneer character, a two-dimensional swinger called the King of Hearts, and a know-it-all detective. Avery's rubber face and mime techniques had him portraying a monk, a Mike Nichols sophisticate at a cocktail party, and a psychiatrist's patient who thinks he is a balloon and visibly deflates as his shrink (Jack) says, "Let's try to pinpoint your problem." But the series did not work out the same way Rowan and Martin's summer show did. It ran thirteen weeks and vanished.

Jack Burns (l.) and Avery Schreiber (r.) doing the "Cab Driver" routine in the late 60s. (*Courtesy Jack Burns*)

The special had been nominated for an Emmy and won a Writers' Guild award, but somehow the series did not match up. Part of it was due to ABC's position as number three in a three-network system; the show was not carried by a number of the ABC affiliates. They also kept pushing Burns and Schreiber to be more commercial, which led to hassles and a diluted version of their style. The team went back to clubs but the Vegas audience was only ready for their humor when they had weekly television exposure. They tried to make the act more commercial but it wasn't what they wanted to do. Jack Burns says that he is not a stand-up comic. The act broke up in 1974 and Jack Burns has not performed much since that time.

Jack devoted himself to writing full-time and has logged producer and head writer credits on "The Glen Campbell Show," "Hee Haw," "The Julie Andrews Hour" and "The Flip Wilson Show." While doing other series and specials he worked with Anthony Newley and Leslie Briscusse adapting the script of *Peter Pan* for TV. In London (1976) he wrote and produced a show featuring Jim Henson's Muppets. "The Muppet Show," which Avery guested on, earned Jack an Emmy nomination in 1977. That same year his Broadway play *Tricks* had its world premiere and he became producer-writer on a new CBS sitcom called "We've Got Each Other." After the demise of "We've Got Each Other," Jack went on to script the movie version of the muppets, "The Muppet Movie."

Avery has been described as "all four Marx brothers at once." His roles have varied as widely as Mr. Evil in a children's TV series called "The Popcorn Machine" to Sir Toby Belch in Shakespeare's *Twelfth Night*. He played the gravedigger in *Hamlet* and the lead in Ben Jonson's *Volpone* at the Mark Taper in Los Angeles. His last Broadway show was David Merrick's *Dreyfuss in Rehearsal* with Ruth Gordon and old vaudevillian Sam Levine. In their other classic routine, Avery played a very human subway vending machine that, for a price, gives advice: "Know why people don't like you, buddy? It's because . . . click . . . whwhwhiiiiirrrrr . . . Please insert another quarter." His latest venture is adviser for a bank that wants to humanize its completely mechanical teller machines. He also has an album out ("The Watergate Comedy Hour"), two recent films (*Swashbuckler* and Marty Feldman's *Last Remake of Beau Geste*) and is embarking on a one-man show that will incorporate mime, sketches, music, and stand-up humor. Avery continues to make TV appearances and perform in stage plays in L.A. He also has a local comedy workshop in Hollywood.

Jack Burns and Avery Schreiber delved a little deeper. They were actors with distinct gifts—Jack taking the route of the time to writing, Avery reverting to his roots as a mime and improv comedian. They furthered the advance of sketches or playlets and then gave way to their separate needs. When Rowan and Martin went off the air Burns and Schreiber were the hottest team around, at least on TV and in clubs. The possibility of the two men reteaming is remote but they have a definite place in the great comedy teams.

The Written Laugh (Clair and McMahon)

Elaine May directs and writes films; Dick Martin writes and directs TV sitcoms; Jack Burns produces and writes television and film comedy. The trend of the sixties comedy teams was to turn from acting to comedy and from comedy performance to comedy writing and sometimes direction. The evolution is most clearly defined in Dick Clair and Jenna McMahon. They were actors first, then a comedy team and, although still performing on occasion, they have been a successful comedy writing team since 1970.

Like Nichols and May, who influenced them, they are not married, and like Reiner and Brooks they are from a similar religious background. There are a number of comedy teams in which all (whether two or more) of the members are Jewish: Smith and Dale, the Marx Brothers, Nichols and May, Reiner and Brooks. But, except for the short teaming of Jack Burns and George Carlin, Clair and McMahon are the only team in which both members are Catholic.

Having some improvisational experience, Clair and Mc-Mahon are actors and their routines are set. They do satirical material but avoid anything topical. They prefer doing comedy that is just as effective with a different President in office. They generally do characters in "small tension situations": a couple on vacation with six kids in the back seat; a talk-show interview with a tap-dancing nun; a couple who are attracted to each other while censoring material for an antismut society.

HE: This first magazine is entitled *Peekaboo*. Nothing but photographs of young ladies in the nude.
SHE: Well, I don't see any redeeming cultural significance, do you?
HE: Well . . . the color tones are very rich.

Even though people "still think she's Clair [Jenna]," Richard Clair Jones was born in San Francisco in the thirties. Sometime after the early thirties, Dick attended a Catholic high school. He then got an M.A. in English from a Catholic university (Loyola) in Los Angeles:

DICK: I saw my first girl when I graduated from college.
JENNA: She was a nun.

Mary Virginia Skinner was born in 1933 in Kansas City, Missouri, and began doing "plays" in the neighborhood as

Clair (l.) and McMahon (r.) discussing why all of those dots
keep them awake (early 70s). (*Courtesy Dick Clair*)

a child. While Dick was watching a lot of movies and flunk-
ing his second-class Scout test, Virginia was doing Greta
Garbo. After high school she studied acting in New York
with Stella Adler in the mid-fifties and did about twenty
Off-Broadway plays as well as the national company of *A
Member of the Wedding* which starred Ethel Waters and
Julie Harris. She was a dramatic actress and was frequently
on the early TV dramas like "Lux Theater" and "Studio
One." In 1959 she moved to Los Angeles and created her

own theater, the Cameo Playhouse. She directed, produced, handled the box office, swept up, and rewrote plays.

Dick got out of the army and immediately spent one whole week just introducing himself to girls. He had been in a lot of plays in college and headed for New York and acting workshops. He did some Off-Off-Broadway plays. He also did some bit parts on television. During his years in New York he held down some of the choicest jobs in the city— waiter, ticket tearer at a movie house, and a peanut salesman. He moved back to Los Angeles in the early sixties and began teaching high school. He never abandoned acting and did small roles on TV, winding up with a recurring role on the "Dobie Gillis" series. He wrote some unproduced teleplays and movie treatments and in 1962 brought a play to the Cameo Playhouse.

Script in hand, he encountered Jenna. She told him to draw up some advertisements for the next play at the theater and he promptly did. Jenna was keeping the Cameo going, writing original material and teaching acting. They both appeared in the next play, *The Man in the Dog Suit*, in 1963. Dick and Jenna then formed an improvisation group at the Cameo which eventually turned out an original revue which they acted in and wrote. After the revue opened in 1965 and ran for a while, the idea of taking some of the material and adapting it to a comedy act dawned on them.

For the next year or so they learned the technique of playing nightclubs while perfecting their act. They played small clubs around L.A. like the Ice House in Pasadena and Ye Little Club in Beverly Hills. At first they attacked the audience with five hundred props and kept forgetting to talk into the microphones. But they started to get the hang of it and in 1967 progressed from local coffeehouses to the Purple Onion in San Francisco, where the Smothers Brothers got their start. They auditioned for Art Linkletter's talent

scouts and sent the film to the Merv Griffin show in New York.
The Griffin representative told them they could be on the
show when they were in New York—they were in New York
within a week. They did a number of Griffin shows and,
as a result, Johnny Carson's show and Ed Sullivan's. Their
club dates picked up with Basin Street East in New York,
Mr. Kelly's in Chicago, the Shoreham Hotel in Washington,
and the Playboy Club circuit.

By 1968 their network shows started executives thinking.
In 1969 they did an ABC variety hour ("What's It All About,
World?") that starred Dean Jones. The following year they
starred with four other couples in "The Funny Side," a re-
vue/sketch show. Neither series lasted longer than thirteen
weeks. While their team career flourished, they took the
writing they did for their act and changed it into situation
comedy writing. Their first assignment was a segment of
"The Mary Tyler Moore Show" and they went on to write
more episodes. They also wrote for "Maude," "The Paul
Lynde Show," "The Bob Newhart Show" (long before Dick
Martin joined the staff), and Dick Van Dyke's second series.

In 1972 they were doing less and less performing and
more and more writing. Like Patchett and Tarses, who never
made it as an act but have been very successful as a writing
team, Clair and McMahon became fixtures on TV as comedy
scripters. They became permanent staff writers on "The
Carol Burnett Show" and have remained there, winning six
Emmy nominations and two Emmys for writing. They wrote
various skits and sketches for Carol, but they are most known
for "Eunice and Ed" or the "Family," which was a down-
home, Midwestern family. They still fit in appearances as a
team on "Dinah" or one of Dean Martin's shows and they
have been preparing an album for a while. But their main
thrust is writing: TV projects (like sitcom pilot "Back
Home"), a book on the Burnett sketches, and a film ro-
mance about an exhibitionist entitled *I See London, I See*

Dick Clair (l.) has just said something lascivious to Jenna McMahon (r.) during a sketch in the 70s. (*Courtesy Dick Clair*)

France. After the Burnett show went off the air they penned a TV film for Carol from Erma Bombeck's best-seller *The Grass Is Always Greener Over the Septic Tank.*

Clair and McMahon's comedy is away from the mainstream of satire that permeates most teams of the sixties. Their humor is not topical and is geared more toward TV; hence, their success as writers in that medium. They seem to round out one path of the sixties and seventies comedy teams. The other path is quite different.

The Gold Glitter, Hard Rock, Freaked-out, Bad-mouth Wackos of the 70s (Cheech and Chong)

Clowns look funny. They make people laugh without saying a word. Silent film comedians wore exaggerated costumes and had a slightly silly appearance. Laurel and Hardy looked funny. The same was true of vaudeville and talking film comics; the Marx Brothers were a funny-looking group. Burns and Allen were unusual. They were a "patter" team and didn't need to look funny. Later, only the comic in the team looked funny (Lou Costello, Jerry Lewis) and the straight man did not (Bud Abbott, Dean Martin). Subsequent to Martin and Lewis, there was little visual differentiation between the straight man and the comic (the Smothers Brothers, Rowan and Martin). In the '60s the majority of comedy teams were comic actors assuming manifold roles. Marty Allen of Allen and Rossi had an outlandish hairdo; Avery Schreiber had bushy hair and added a silent film mustache. But most of the teams looked like average people, not freaks, not funny people.

A beat-up 1949 Mercury, its front bumper on the ground, its trunk high in the air, careens over the curb into a front yard. A spinner hubcap pops off and the dice hanging from the rear-view mirror swing back and forth. A funny-looking guy gets out. He is a Chicano, has long hair down to his shoulders and a large mustache. He nervously looks around. He is wearing a head band and beads, scruffy Levi's and a long vest, but no shirt. He tries to look cool as he weaves up to the front door of an apartment. He knocks on the door secretively.

> *KNOCK, KNOCK, KNOCK.*
> *(PAUSE)*
> *KNOCK, KNOCK, KNOCK.*
> *(PAUSE) FROM INSIDE:*

Wow. Who is it?

> *THE MAN OUTSIDE, ANXIOUS:*

It's Dave. Let me in.

> *(PAUSE)*

Dave's not here, man.

I know man. *I'M Dave, man!* I've got the stuff and I think someone followed me.

> *(PAUSE)*

Dave?

Yeh! Dave! Now let me in, man.

> *(PAUSE)*

. . . Dave's not here, man.

The "stuff" is marijuana. The guy inside who is so gone he doesn't get what is going on is Chong. The guy playing Dave is Cheech. They look funny and they sound funny.

The satiric tone of the sixties humor reflected a change in society. Young people were fans of Lenny Bruce and the Smothers Brothers and Mort Sahl. Those young people who were against the war in Vietnam, who thought everyone over thirty was a hypocrite, grew up on satire, hard rock, dirty words and dope (marijuana). As they moved into their thirties, most of them blended into society out of necessity or simply by the idealism of youth giving way to the conservatism of age.

The new counterculture is less concerned about moral values, right and wrong, helping the underprivileged. But they still cherish hard rock, they still use swear words that are unacceptable to their parents and older folks, and, if they don't smoke marijuana, they certainly know a great deal about it.

It was 1971. Lenny Bruce had been dead for a number of years; the Smothers Brothers had been silenced by the networks; Rowan and Martin were doing the same things; Stiller and Meara were apart; Nichols and May had not been a team for almost ten years; Mort Sahl was not seen often and was mellowing; Clair and McMahon were writing for TV and Burns and Schreiber were doing singles; Bob and Ray did not appeal to hard rock types; Reiner and Brooks were phantoms. Enter Cheech and Chong.

This comedy team immediately became superstars of the counterculture. Cheech and Chong weren't very young (in 1971 they were respectively twenty-five and thirty-two), they didn't harp on war or the failings of the Establishment—they just put everybody on. They both look like two "down" dudes, freaked-out on drugs, who are constantly forgetting things like their names or that TV sets are blank until you turn them on. The kids who were growing up while the Vietnam war and the social hullabaloo of the sixties were winding down just wanted to laugh and identify with symbols of things they were, of things they did and liked: rock music, Levi's, drugs, sex, the easy, simple life. Chong: "We don't have any blatant messages and they seem to like us for that. And they like us because we're crazy." Cheech: "We deal with the same human frailties but in a different environmental condition—drugs and relaxed social mores."

Thomas (Tommy) Chong was born in Edmonton, Alberta (Canada), in 1939 to a Chinese truckdriver and his Scotch-Irish-French wife. He grew up in Calgary and considers his Chinese heritage as incidental to his Canadian environment. He played guitar and sang rhythm and blues early, getting his first pro gig at sixteen in 1955. He joined Bobby Taylor and the Vancouvers and the group was signed to Motown Records. On the road, he co-wrote a hit, "Does Your Mama Know?" and managed to catch the Second City in Chicago and the Committee in San Francisco. When the group disbanded he returned to Vancouver to direct "stage shows" at a topless club owned by his family.

Richard Marin (Cheech) was born in 1946 in Watts, a Los Angeles ghetto. He came from a large family and his father was a sergeant on the Los Angeles police force. Richard's nickname Cheech is short for *cheecharone*, which is Spanish for deep-fried pork (crackling). The family moved to a white suburb and Cheech started singing with big-name groups like Rompin' Richie and the Rockin' Rubins and the ever-popular Captain Shagnasty and his Loch Ness Pickles. He finished a college degree by dishwashing and working as a janitor. He even harbored the middle-class goal of being a lawyer, a goal that he shared with another comedian: Groucho Marx. But he found what he wanted, for a while, by becoming a potter and working in clay. Like a number of other young American men at the time, he finished college and sped to Canada to avoid the draft. Once safe, he continued molding clay, delivered carpets, and worked as a cook in a large hotel.

Before leaving the hotel, Cheech broke his leg and, brandishing the knee-to-ankle pin, qualified as 4-F. Chong, meanwhile, had dropped the topless dancers in his club. He opted for a more conservative show replacing the topless dancers with an unusual improvisation group. The group, called City Works, consisted of a mime artist, blackouts, jokes about sex and drugs, "hip burlesque," and four topless actresses. Cheech, meanwhile, connected with rock star Frank Zappa and cut an album. From that strangeness he happened onto Vancouver and the only seminude, improv freak show in the

Tommy Chong (l.) and Richard Marin (Cheech, r.) of Cheech and Chong on a concert tour in their 1908 Edsel sedan. (*Courtesy Paul Wasserman*)

world. Cheech had hung around the Instant Theater (a local improv group) in L.A. for about a month but that was the extent of his acting-comedy career.

Cheech saw the strange happenings onstage and joined in instantly. The two started developing a straight man (Chong) comic (Cheech) rapport within the burlesque structure. The group began taking audience suggestions like all of the well-known improvisational units. The only difference was that City Works played to hockey players, drunks, kids, truckdrivers, and loggers. City Works had a good following and hung on for a while. Then the group split up. Cheech and Chong tried working with two women, but that did not make it. When they could get work, they did gigs with rock bands in western Canada. The act developed and evolved at this time into what it presently is—sketches that have no distinct straight man and no distinct comic. Both Cheech and Chong play comic and straight man.

It was 1969, the end of a decade, the beginning of another. The duo played a coffeehouse and decided that was their kind of action. They headed for Los Angeles. But they did not hit paydirt at the Ice House in Pasadena. It took time for the act to get polished and for them to catch on. They ranged from freebies, like talent night at Red Foxx's joint, to discotheques, and from black audiences at the Climax to hitting the Troubadour on Monday mornings, hanging around to be first to audition. They finally clicked at the Troubadour and were signed to do an album.

In late '71 they cut their first album, "Cheech and Chong." Lou Adler, the head of Ode Records, saw them perform at a "hoot" night at the Troub and signed them to a contract. A hoot night is a night when musicians, singers, and comics perform their material for free, hoping to get discovered. The first album sold. Cheech and Chong started getting known and played the Bitter End in New York and clubs from Chicago to Detroit to Dallas. As their first album started to turn gold they cut "Big Bambu" in '72 and it began overtaking the first disc. "Big Bambu" was the number one comedy album in '72; "Cheech and Chong" was only number two that year.

Since that time they have given concerts all over the nation, including one at Carnegie Hall with rock group Sha Na Na; they have cut six albums, the third being "Los Cochinos" ("The Pigs") and the fourth "Cheech and Chong's Wedding Album." Their first three albums are all gold, the first selling a million, the second and third a million and a half each. "Los Cochinos" also won the '73 Grammy Award and the "Wedding Album" was "shipped

gold" (it was presold in excess of a million dollars). The
fifth album is "Sleeping Beauty"; the sixth is the sound
track from their film "Up in Smoke."

But the team has done only one or two TV shows, and
those in Canada. Television is not ready for two freaks who
talk openly about sex and drugs. But as Chong points out,
the tube was not ready for Archie Bunker either—until Norman Lear put the network on the spot and they tried the
show. As the mores of the country and television change,
Cheech and Chong are becoming less outrageous and more
like a youthful (in their thirties), hip, middle-class comedy
team.

Cheech and Chong have their first movie in release. Their
film was variously reported in *Variety*, the show-business
magazine, as being released by at least two studios (it is a
Paramount release, the same studio that did the Martin and
Lewis films), and had numerous titles: *The Adventures of
Pedro and the Man, Cheech and Chong's Greatest Hits,
Greatest Hits*, and *Cheech and Chong*.

The film, produced and directed by Lou Adler and written by Tommy and Richard, was finally called *Up in Smoke*.
It has a rather simple plot "similar to Abbott and Costello."
The supporting cast includes Edie Adams, Stacey Keach, Jr.,
Strother Martin, and Tom Skerrit. It was questionable for a
while whether the film would ever be finished or edited or
seen in final print. *Up in Smoke* is the first comedy team film
since Rowan and Martin's *The Maltese Bippy* almost ten
years ago in 1969 (excluding British team Monty Python
and the National Lampoon movie, which does not really
feature a team). The film is a box-office hit to the tune of over
$40,000,000 in the first four months of release. It is the first
team comedy movie to be a success since Martin and Lewis
made their last film in 1956, more than twenty years ago.

Cheech and Chong are the hottest American comedy
team around in the late seventies, if not the only comedy

team given the sporadic appearances of Rowan and Martin, Stiller and Meara, Bob and Ray, and Clair and McMahon. "The Not Ready for Prime Time Players" on "Saturday Night Live" are only a team by attrition; when the show goes off they will disband. Cheech and Chong incorporate many of the elements that started with Bob and Ray and Nichols and May: they improvise and have done improvisational theater; they satirize the pot-smoking, rock-pulsating young people of the '70s; they play different characters; they don't rely on one-liners very often. On the other hand, they hark back (to use a 2,000-year-old man's phrase) to burlesque, they dress funny like the old-timers, and they are very much identified as Cheech playing a television DJ or Chong parodying an old-time Black blues singer (Blind Melon Chitlin')—they do not become hidden in their characters.

Although they readily admit influences like the improv groups, Lenny Bruce and Richard Pryor, they very definitely steer away from the direct assaults on politics and social values which Lenny, in particular, made. Although they are directed at a hip audience, they are conservative within their hipness. The humor of the sixties has given over to a more fifties-like, uninvolved humor in the seventies.

There are other teams around that are the old style: Gaylord and Holiday, Skyles and Henderson. There are still remnants of the satiric fire of the sixties: the Firesign Theater, the Credibility Gap, and similar groups. There are singles that are more to the point, most pointedly George Carlin, but even Carlin has retreated from his Lenny Bruce position. In 1977 George Carlin played Vegas, where he had been kicked out in 1970, and he was accepted. Part of the acceptance had to do with the change in society and, hence, the generally unhip Vegas audiences. Part of it had to do with George Carlin's mellowing and pulling back from his earlier Smothers Brothers–Lenny Bruce–Mort Sahl stance. But none of the teams that carry over the anxiety and zeal of the sixties are making it big. Only Cheech and Chong are on top. They played Vegas in December 1977 and made twelve appearances (late shows) at the Aladdin Hotel in 1978. The times are changing faster than the comedians.

There was an enormous transition in humor and comedy team humor in the 1960s. It was a revolution that was much like the counterculture revolution. It began with the style of Bob and Ray and was epitomized by Nichols and May. It was taken to one extreme by Tom and Dick Smothers and another by Rowan and Martin. Cheech and Chong are a synthesis of the old and the new, blending satire and burlesque, improvisation and characterization, an attack on social habits, but not on social values.

Nobody knows what the 1980s will bring, but it is a fairly sure bet that very few comedy teams will consist of two guys telling jokes—one a straight man, one a comic.

CHAPTER **9**

Just for the Record

The tendency in the 1970s is to take a male and a female, usually young singers (Donny and Marie Osmond) or young mime-dancers (Shields and Yarnell) or slightly older singers (Sonny and Cher), and try to make them into a comedy team. It just does not work. Whatever the failings of the slapstick nonsense the Three Stooges recorded on film, and which is still being aired on TV, there is more comedy in one of their ten-minute shorts than a whole season of the man and woman singers and dancers.

Donald O'Connor and Sydney Miller were an on-and-off comedy team for years, especially in clubs, but they never made it big as a team. Bob Hope and Bing Crosby did seven films together but they were known separately and never really constituted a team. Joseph Bologna and Renee Taylor are both actors and writers and they collaborate. But they never made it as an act. Fibber McGee and Molly were enormously popular and important as a radio team but they faded as the medium faltered. Amos and Andy were even more important. The "Amos 'n' Andy" show was the first large hit on radio and ran from 1928 to 1954. Freeman F. Gosden played Amos and Charles J. Correll was Andy. Both were white men playing Black characters, so when the show was moved to television Black actors had to take over the roles. But Gosden and Correll cannot be left out of the great comedy teams.

Trying to decide what teams to include and what teams to exclude is a touchy business, especially when vaudeville was at its height. Weber and Fields, Clark and McCollough, Wheeler and Woolsey, Olsen and Johnson, the Wiere Brothers, Van and Schenck, Ham and Bud, Fric and Frac—the list goes on and on. It is easy to delete a team like Clayton, Jackson and Durante since they were not together long and they did not make a dent in the long line rising to top billing. (One of the members, Jimmy Durante, did.) It is much harder to leave out the Ritz Brothers (Al, Jimmy, and Harry), particularly when Harry has been lauded by almost everyone in the comedy field. Mel Brooks called Harry the funniest man alive. After Al died in 1962, the two surviving brothers started a comeback and were seen frequently on Joey Bishop's talk show in the late sixties. But the Ritz Brothers were visual comedians first, verbal comedians second.

The oldest living member of a comedy team is Joe Smith, who is ninety-four. Smith and Dale performed as a team for seventy years (1898–1968). For that reason and because their material is still effective, Smith and Dale will represent the host of vaudeville comedians who teamed up and went on to do movies, radio, and television.

Dr. Kronkhite and His Only Living Patient (Smith and Dale)

In 1898 on the Lower East Side of New York City, far removed from the ongoing fighting of the Spanish–American War, a fourteen-year-old boy named Joe rented a bicycle. Charlie, a sixteen-year-old boy, had also rented a bike and proceeded up Eldridge Street. At Delancey and Eldridge the two bikers collided and a crowd gathered, expecting a fight.

Instead of throwing blows, the two boys got up, examined their mutual damage, and started off to return the mangled two-wheelers.

Joe began walking his bent bike back to the rental shop. So did Charlie. Joe noticed that Charlie was behind him, so he turned around and shouted, "What are you following me for?" Charlie shot back, "I'm not following you. You're walking ahead of me." This started a feeling of camaraderie and they continued wisecracking back and forth. The owner of the bike store thought they sounded like Weber and Fields, one of the biggest comedy teams at the turn of the century. He gave them a tandem bicycle for free, and a few weeks later the team of Marks and Sultzer was rehearsing.

Charlie Marks was born in 1881 and Joe Sultzer in 1884. They both grew up in New York and at the time of their collision-course meeting Joe was a shipping clerk, while Charlie was apprenticed to a printer. They met in 1898 and began performing that year. They continued doing the act until 1968, their last appearance being at the Lamb's Club in midtown Manhattan. The Lamb's is one of the two American clubs exclusively made up of stage actors.

They rehearsed in the Weber and Fields music hall and even caught the attention of the then top bananas of vaudeville, Joe Weber and Lew Fields. Weber and Fields had a profound effect on Joe and Charlie. "Dr. Kronkhite," their best-remembered routine, was originally done in a German dialect, which was the specialty of Weber and Fields. Dialect humor was in vogue, given the blend of languages that the new immigrants brought to America. The favorites were Italian (Chico Marx), Irish, Jewish (Groucho Marx), Dutch, and German.

Originally emanating from the South, blackface comedy was also the style. White men applied burnt cork to their faces and a big team like Moran and Mack were originally billed with their real names as "Smith and Dale, Blackface

Singing and Dancing Comedians." Then they decided to change their names to Moran and Mack and later to "The Two Black Crows." When they opted for the name change, a printer was stuck with all of their old posters saying Smith and Dale. Joe Sultzer's brother got the posters and Marks and Sultzer became (Joe) Smith and (Charlie) Dale.

They played saloons and beer halls in the Bowery and Chinatown as Sultzer and Marks or Marks and Sultzer, and danced more than they joked. Almost all comedians danced and/or sang in vaudeville: Laurel and Hardy both danced and sang, George Burns sang and did a soft-shoe routine with Gracie, and the Marx Brothers incorporated music into their act even when they went on to films. Joe and Charlie were also capable acrobats, like Mitchell and Durant, a team that later made acrobatic falls their stamp. Joe and Charlie moved up to Child's restaurant and, with their name change, played the Atlantic Garden and the Palace Garden. They finally began touring, and the act changed to mostly comedy.

While on the road they had the ill fortune to play San Francisco during the 1906 earthquake. They also accidentally fell into a practice that was not revived until much later. The radio and later TV comics were all identified with their sponsors, but it took Bob and Ray in the mid-fifties to put a new twist on the commercial advertisement plug— they satirized the products and then started making commercials under the auspices of their own company. Smith and Dale arrived at their commercial boon in a roundabout way. One of their dialogue exchanges was:

SMITH: Name two of the principal oceans.
DALE: Atlantic and Pacific.
SMITH: No, that's a tea company.

They used the short bit for three years, thinking the famous tea company wouldn't mind. But one night a lawyer cornered them backstage. They apologized and promised not to

do the lines anymore but the lawyer urged them to continue, giving them $25 a week to keep it in the act. They
tried to expand the enterprise with another plug:

SMITH: Give me a sentence with the word "delight" in it.
DALE: De wind blew in de window and blew out de light.
SMITH: Give me a sentence with "deliver" in it.
DALE: Carter's little [liver] pills are good for de liver.

Smith and Dale had connected with two other comedians
and became the Avon Comedy Four. Around the same time
as the Frisco quake, the "Dr. Kronkhite" routine began to
emerge. This routine lasted throughout their career and
was varied continually. It wasn't developed into a full routine
until 1914. They changed it when there was anti-German
feeling during World War I and continued to update it until
it was used on the Ed Sullivan show in the 1960s. Some of the
sketch goes like this.

PATIENT: *(Joe Smith)*: . . . Is the doctor in?
NURSE: Yes, but he's very busy.
PATIENT: I'll wait.
NURSE: Take a chair, please.
PATIENT: Thank you. I'll take it on my way out.
    (Nurse exits. Doctor (Charlie Dale) enters. He skips over to
    patient.)
PATIENT: *(A bit skeptical)* Are you a doctor?
DOCTOR: Yes.
PATIENT: I'm dubious.
DOCTOR: How do you do, Mr. Dubious. . . . Mr. Dubious, are you
  married?
PATIENT: Yes and no.
DOCTOR: What do you mean, yes and no?
PATIENT: I am, but I wish I wasn't . . . you see, I'm my wife's
  step-husband. He stepped out and I stepped in.
DOCTOR: Do you carry any insurance?

PATIENT: Not one penny.

DOCTOR: If you should kick the bucket, what'll your wife bury you with?

PATIENT: With pleasure.

DOCTOR: Well, that's that. Now, what's the matter with you?

PATIENT: I'm sick as a dog.

DOCTOR: You came to the right place. I'm also a veterinarian.

DOCTOR: . . . What troubles you?

PATIENT: Bursitis and it's on the back of my neck. That's a bad place.

DOCTOR: Where would you want a better place than on the back of your neck?

PATIENT: On the back of your neck. And I got a corn on the bottom of my foot. That's a bad spot, no?

DOCTOR: Yes, it's a good spot because nobody can step on it but you.

DOCTOR: . . . Now keep your mouth open and say, fish.

PATIENT: Herring.

DOCTOR: Stick out your tongue. More. More!

PATIENT: I can't, it's tied on the back. Well?

DOCTOR: I've seen better tongues hanging in a delicatessen window. Now, how do you sleep?

PATIENT: *(Closes his eyes and crosses his arms.)* Like this.

DOCTOR: You don't get me.

PATIENT: I don't want you.

DOCTOR: *(Jumping up and down.)* Please! Don't aggravate me. I got no patience.

PATIENT: I shouldn't be here either.

DOCTOR: I asked you how you sleep at night?

PATIENT: At night I can't sleep. I walk around all night.

DOCTOR: Oh. You're a sonnambulance.

PATIENT: No. I'm a night watchman.

PATIENT: . . . What do I owe you?

DOCTOR: Ten dollars.

PATIENT: For what?

DOCTOR: Ten dollars for my advice.

PATIENT: Here's two dollars. Take it, doctor. That's my advice.

DOCTOR: You're nothing but a cheap, low-down, addlepated, first-class insignificant . . .

PATIENT: One more word from you and you'll only get a dollar.

DOCTOR: *You* . . .

PATIENT: That's the word. Here's the dollar. Goodbye.

The Avon Four stayed together fifteen years, making their Broadway debut (1916) in *Why Worry*, starring Fanny Brice, the comedienne-singer portrayed by Barbra Streisand in *Funny Girl*. Three years later the act disbanded and Smith and Dale went back to working as a twosome. They played the vaudeville houses, did Broadway revues, and even

Joe Smith (l.) and Charley Dale (r.) in the 1940s doing their well known "Hungarian Rhapsody" routine. (*Courtesy Joe Smith*)

moved over to the burlesque stage. Charlie had been established as the straight man much earlier, and although they
each did set-up lines, Joe got most of the punch lines. The
team went on, revamping their standard sketches like "A
Hungarian Rhapsody" (which contained Dr. Kronkhite),
"La Schnapps, Inc." and "S.S. Malaria," putting together
new bits and recording some of their visual gags in silent
shorts. In 1929 when the Marx Brothers were riding high on
Broadway and the country was hanging low during the Depression, they joined the lists of old-timers doing talking
shorts for Paramount. They did a few for Warner Brothers,
too.

Abbott and Costello are not nearly as funny as the Marx
Brothers or Burns and Allen or Laurel and Hardy. But a person who cannot laugh at their "Who's on First" routine is
not a true fan of comedy. Smith and Dale used the same
material or the same type of material during all their years
as a comedy team. As they began to make films they were
criticized in the same fashion as Abbott and Costello were
throughout Bud and Lou's entire career: It's old stuff, it's
old hat. It happened to Joe and Charlie before there was an
Abbott and Costello team, but the detractors did not look
for the truth behind the need for "new" things. Mel Brooks,
Steve Martin, Woody Allen, "Laugh In," and Cheech and
Chong do burlesque bits. Sometimes it is funny, sometimes
it is not, but you cannot dismiss it by saying that it is old.
If something is truly funny it doesn't matter if it's old.

The criticism did not stop Smith and Dale, or bother them
much. They did their biggest Broadway hit, *Mendel, Inc.*
in the early 1930s. Ethnic humor was on the wane then so
when Warners filmed the show in 1932 they retitled it *The
Heart of New York.* Warner Brothers' studio was smart
enough not to change the show. After the film they continued
in Broadway revues and began doing radio. Some of their

bigger stage hits were *The Sky's the Limit* and *Crazy Quilt*. They did some shorter, two-reel comedies for Columbia in 1939 like *Mutiny on the Body* with silent film star Charlie Chase.

Things slackened for Smith and Dale in the 1940s. They never made the big time in films and the forties was the era in which movies drowned the last vestiges of burlesque and did a good job on radio; movies were soon to be deluged by television. It was also the era that saw Abbott and Costello become the biggest comedy team in the business via films. Bud and Lou were so big that (Wally) Brown and (Alan) Carney, two vaudeville comics who had become contract players at RKO Radio Pictures, were thrown together as competitors. Brown and Carney made a number of films but never troubled Abbott and Costello. When Martin and Lewis overtook Bud and Lou in the early 1950s, two teams tried to compete with them, with (Duke) Mitchell and (Sammy) Petrillo trying to look like Dean and Jerry and doing an impersonation of them. The other competitors were (Tommy) Noonan and (Peter) Marshall.

But Smith and Dale continued to work as a team. In 1951 they tried again in Hollywood with *Two Tickets to Broadway*. They did a number of their own bits and were the best thing in the rather mediocre film, but it did not lead to more cinematic work. The Palace Theater, which had been the ultimate in vaudeville, attempted a comeback in the same year as *Two Tickets to Broadway* was released. Smith and Dale were the featured act on the Palace's two-a-day bill.

The team again faded for a short time. Both men were approaching their seventies. In 1952 Judy Garland played the Palace for twenty weeks and made a point of booking Smith and Dale on the bill with her. In the late fifties they continued to do revues off and on and started a series of appearances on Ed Sullivan's show that lasted into the late sixties. After Joe's second wife died and he moved into the Actors' Fund home in Englewood, New Jersey, Charlie—dispelling rumors about their arguments—moved into the home, too. Joe continues to live there and Charlie did until he became ill and was moved to a nursing home. A few months later, in 1971, he died at the age of ninety.

Smith and Dale exemplified the vaudeville comedy team through and through. They were the question and answer men that most teams, excluding Laurel and Hardy and the Marx Four, patterned themselves on until the 1960s. And, more important, their material holds up. They developed their own routines—comedians using writers was not the norm until films, radio, and television changed this—using the old form of improvisation, trial and error, and ad libs. But once the bit was set, at least the nucleus remained relatively the same. For years.

Smith and Dale will be remembered for many things but most people don't know that they changed the Sunday blue laws in New York City. In 1906 blue laws prohibited drinking, dancing, and other "lewd behavior" on Sundays. In a letter, Joe Smith describes how they changed the law.

It was in or about 1906 while playing Hammerstein's on 42nd and Broadway doing the school act. Willie Hammerstein, Oscar the 2nd's father, who ran the theatre at the time asked us to do our full Sunday night and that we would be arrested [sic], this would be a tool to try to do away with the Sunday Blue Laws—when a performer couldn't do his comedy act or dancing or an act with scenery or any acrobatics. Well, after doing our full act, a detective came up from the audience and told us to get our makeup off, put on our street clothes and come with him—at the 47th St. Police Station, Willie bailed us out and the trial was held at the 54th St. courthouse the next day and was full of New York managers. The judge asked the detective to explain the case which was called New York City vs. The Avon Comedy Four.

The detective tried to explain the act which was a slapstick act with songs and dancing and then he came to a few of the lines like:

Teacher—Next lesson is spellink.

Pupil—I.N.K., ink.

Teacher—I said spellink is the lesson, not you should spell ink. Spell the word delight.

The judge is leaning over to get the drift. The detective is a West Side hick and using the word "fag" to describe the sissy boy who wears red stockings. . . . [A stock character in the "school" routines.]

Teacher—Now, students, what is the first thing that turns green in the Springtime?

Pupils—Christmas jewelry.

The judge banged his gavel on the desk. "That's enough!" he shouted, "Discharged, case dismissed . . . they have NO ACT!"

So Smith and Dale were the instigators of freedom on Sunday in New York.

Joe Smith is now ninety-four and is still able. He is the oldest living member of the longest lasting comedy team in history. If he and Charlie squabbled, at least they made up long enough to more than rival the shorter lasting and often fighting team of Gilbert and Sullivan, the nineteenth-century operetta composers. Joe still recalls the days with Sophie Tucker, Eddie Cantor, Ed Wynn, and Fannie Brice. He still remembers routines. In 1972 Neil Simon's *The Sunshine Boys* arrived on Broadway. The play is modeled on an old vaudeville team and it is fairly obvious that Smith and Dale were the models. The two old teammates in the play even appear on the Ed Sullivan show and do a doctor bit in Act II.

The play was made into a film starring Walter Matthau and another comedy team member, George Burns, in 1974. Burns won his only Oscar for acting in the film in 1975, at the age of eighty. But then he's just a kid.

White on Black (Amos 'n' Andy)

There are three things I'll never forget about America: the
Rocky Mountains, Niagara Falls, and Amos and Andy.
                                    —GEORGE BERNARD SHAW

The Puzzles of 1925 features a baritone named Walter
Pidgeon. Mary Hay is doing a dance act with Clifton Webb.
Oscar Levant is playing piano in an orchestra at the
Rialto Theater, New York. An ex-swimming champ and
hoofer gets his first speaking role in *Outside Looking In,* a
Broadway play. His name is James Cagney. George Raft is
called the "fastest Charleston dancer" in *Variety*. The Loew's
State Theater bill has an act on in the number two spot that
consists of a little dancing, some songs, and an imitation of
Eddie Cantor. The star of the act goes by the unlikely
name of Milton Berle. Charles Correll plays piano and Freeman Gosden the ukulele in a revue called *Red Hot*. Three
years later, Gosden and Correll would make history as
"Amos 'n' Andy."

"Amos 'n' Andy" was probably the most popular radio
show ever broadcast. It reached over 40 million people long
before the intricate and elaborate hook-ups of television
came along. Movie houses stopped their films at seven
o'clock so "Amos 'n' Andy" could be piped in; newspapers
gave daily accounts of the show when Amos went on trial
for murder; from seven to seven-fifteen there were more auto
thefts than at any other time of day and people used less
water for that quarter of an hour. The show was a phenomenon that has only been equaled in recent years and had
never been approached before 1928. Perhaps the closest recent event would be the 1976 showing of "Roots" on television. But that was only for eight straight days. "Amos 'n'
Andy" lasted from 1928 to 1954. George Bernard Shaw
listened; J. Edgar Hoover listened; Herbert Hoover listened.

The television version of the show in 1954 never achieved as huge a following and was short-lived, due to the controversy over the style of the show. The roles on "Amos 'n' Andy" (Amos, the Kingfish, Andy, Lightnin', Ruby, Madam Queen, Brother Crawford) were stereotypes of certain rural Blacks from the South. When the show hit TV in the fifties with characters saying things like "An' dat's de trufe . . . I'ze regusted . . . 'Splain it to me . . ." the Black community charged that the show was an insult and a disgrace to their race. The NAACP filed a formal protest. The new sense of the Black person's image that was ushered in by the civil protests of the fifties brought an end to "Amos 'n' Andy." That show was not the only one criticized. The film *Gone With the Wind* was condemned along with a number of other popular books, movies, and plays. But "Amos 'n' Andy" went off the air and changed from national heroes into villains. The subject is still sensitive. A comedy series called "Taxi" that premiered in fall 1978 was originally supposed to be based on the "Fresh Air Taxi Co." of Amos 'n' Andy. It was changed to represent a cross-section of people who were almost all Caucasian.

Charles J. Correll (Andy) was born in 1890 in Peoria, Illinois, the same city that produced the hottest Black comedian of the seventies, Richard Pryor. Correll's family was from the South but, like many, they moved north during the Reconstruction period. He was a stonemason, a stenographer, and a pianist. Like Chico Marx, he started in show business playing the piano, only he accompanied silent films in a movie house. He went on to be a dramatic coach for a Chicago company that put on amateur shows across the nation. He toured the country for a while, setting up pageants and amateur theatricals. He was assigned to stage a musical in Durham, North Carolina, for an Elks lodge and, not being able to pull it off alone, was assisted by Freeman F. Gosden. Gosden (Amos) was born in Richmond,

Virginia, in 1899 and was educated in Atlanta. He was a traveling tobacco salesman and sometimes stopped in one place long enough to sell a few cars. At one time in his early career, he was an "egg-bearer" for Thurston the Magician. Gosden was a navy radio operator in World War I and came out of the service determined to make his way in show business. But his only experience had been playing the ukulele as an amateur.

After Charlie and Freeman handled the Elks with aplomb, they decided that they made a pretty good team and continued to work out of Chicago, planning the road seasons of the amateur theatricals, traveling to implement them, sometimes together, sometimes apart. In 1920 they did their first radio broadcast as a performing team—an experimental station in New Orleans wanted to test its equipment. They even cut some "talking records" for Victor that were labeled terrible by one publication but, undaunted, they kept on trying to break in an act. For five years they performed on the side while staging revues and plays out of Chicago. In 1925 they started a regular job singing at the Edgewater Beach Hotel at radio station WEBH, which broadcast live from the penthouse.

When not performing or staging shows they worked on a song and joke act. They incorporated some of the Negro dialect into the routines they did, that being a natural outgrowth of their Southern upbringing. They auditioned the act and got a job on station WGN in Chicago. But they insisted on getting at least $10 a week for their work. They got $125, but they earned it. When they started doing their show in November of 1925 they did a nonstop combination of songs, piano and uke duos and solos, announcements and commercials, and jokes that lasted from 10 A.M. until the following day at 2 A.M. That may seem like a long workday but it was not unusual at the time; people worked much longer hours in 1925. Gosden and Correll had been singing for their meals for eight months, so however long their WGN show, they were pleased to do it. After about three months they were asked to take a comic strip from the *Chicago Tribune* (which owned and ran WGN) and work it into a radio show. They, in turn, suggested a dialogue show with a couple of Black characters. The general manager of the *Tribune* agreed.

In January 1926 "Sam 'n' Henry" became a new show and, soon, a new hit. The show was so well liked that its following grew over the next two years and Correll and Gosden even did a personal appearance tour as Sam and Henry. Finding a better offer of money from station WMAQ, they moved over but were prevented from continuing the show as Sam and Henry. "Sam 'n' Henry" stayed at WGN with two other actors filling in, but it was not the same show and shortly went off the air.

Looking for a new title, the team hit on "Amos 'n' Andy." The show premiered in March 1928 and was soon in demand by other stations. The network set-up of NBC and CBS was very crude at the time. So Gosden and Correll put together their own network consisting of about forty-five stations. The show was doing so well on its own that in 1929 NBC offered them a contract at $100,000 a year, a lot of money in those days and particularly in that Depression year. The show was a hit for the next twenty years.

"Amos 'n' Andy" had over a hundred different characters and Gosden and Correll did them all. They also wrote all of the scripts for the show for the first ten years. Amos Jones and Andrew H. Brown were Black men who lived in Harlem and owned the Fresh Air Taxi Company. The shoestring operation had one beat-up taxi, in worse shape than Jack Benny's later Maxwell, and the fresh air title was the result of a missing windshield. Amos was a hard-working citizen with a wife (Ruby) and two kids; he went to church and was full of goodwill. He was so nice that he did not seem to generate much laughter and, as a result, his role in the show was progressively reduced until by 1943 he only appeared sporadically.

Andy, on the other ear, was everybody's patsy. He chased

Amos 'n' Andy (Charles J. Correll as Andy, l., and Freeman F. Gosden as Amos, r.) in 1938 when their radio show was still at its peak. (*Courtesy Freeman F. Gosden*)

women, smoked old stogies and, his derby in place, was always scheming to get money that he eventually lost, along with some of his own minimal stash. The Mystic Knights of the Sea was a lodge that Amos and Andy belonged to and was much like the Raccoons that Ralph Kramden (Jackie Gleason) and Norton (Art Carney) belonged to in the 1950s TV series "The Honeymooners." George Stevens, alias the Kingfish, was also a member of the lodge and his conniving flamboozling of Andy was the major topic of the show. He would flimflam Andy into buying the Brooklyn Bridge twice in the same day and then get rent for the land it stood on.

Lightnin' was the most objectionable character to most of the later critics, although he was certainly loved by millions the first twenty or so years of the show. Lightnin' was the slowest person alive. He made the character of Pedro, who is so freaked-out on marijuana he can't remember his name, whom Cheech and Chong used in the late 1970s, seem like a debating champion. Sometimes Lightnin' would take two or three programs to dust a vase.

In 1929 people were out of work and not very happy. The Depression was lightened somewhat by the antics of "Amos 'n' Andy." People who couldn't afford to see the Marx Brothers on Broadway could hear Correll and Gosden for nothing. The program had to be broadcast at two different times because of the fans' demands on the opposite coasts. There was no such thing as tape delay; everything was done live. Originally there was no studio audience and Correll and Gosden just worked up a script and put it on. In one script Kingfish needs some money and Andy needs a doctor. Kingfish tells Andy he'll be right over and tells Lightnin' to get a dusty doctor's case out of the closet.

LIGHTNIN': Where yo' git dis?

KINGFISH: I let another doctor have five dollars once, an' he lef dis heah fo' me to hold.

LIGHTNIN': Dat's whut yo' call holdin' de bag, ain't it?

KINGFISH: Now, dis thing heah yo' put in yo' ears an' yo' listen. . . . Dere's de thermomeler. Now, dere's a thing dere. See dis thing heah? Yo' wrap dis round a man's arm an' yo' pump it up an' yo' watch dat speedometer—dat's de blood pressure. . . . On de way over we'll stop and git one o' dem ice-cream things on a stick, an' den I kin use de stick to hold down his tongue when he say "ah."

At Andy's "Dr." Kingfish gets to work:

KINGFISH: . . . Lightnin', where is de ah-stick?

LIGHTNIN': By de way, Kingfish, dis is a lucky stick. Yo' kin git one ice cream fo' nuthin' wid it.

KINGFISH: Yeah? Wait a minute. I got a pencil in my pocket. Open yo' mouth, Andy.
. . . See brother Andy, dis is a stethascope.

LIGHTNIN': Don't yo' want to take his clothes off?

KINGFISH: Dis thing listens through anything. . . . Wait a minute heah. Yo' got a knock in yo' 'pendix. Boy, it's really goin' to town.

ANDY: Yo' is pressin' dat thing on my watch.

KINGFISH: . . . Look heah, Andy. How much money yo' got?

ANDY: Ten dollahs—in de mattress.

KINGFISH: . . . Today's Tuesday. You got ten dollars. Two dollars a treatment. Sat'day yo'll be well.

Kingfish directs Lightnin' to put the "thermomeler" in a bowl of hot water to ensure cleanliness. He then concludes that either the thermometer is not working or Andy is dead.

In 1937 the show lost its original sponsor, quickly gaining another. Gosden and Correll moved their families to the West Coast and continued the show. By 1939, when they did another huge promotion like Amos's murder trial—this time the marriage of Andy—they were making $7,000 a week. In the mid-thirties their audience started being drained off by all of the vaudevillians who had invaded radio in that decade. The new shows were slicker, had bands and laugh-inducing announcers, and played for a live audience. "Amos 'n' Andy" fell from first place to below fifty on the rating system, the victims of Jack Benny, Burns and Allen, Edgar Bergen and Charlie McCarthy, and even Fibber McGee and Molly.

In 1943 they changed formats and did a half-hour show once a week instead of the fifteen minutes, five days a week they had maintained since 1928. By this time they had added a lot of supporting players for the numerous roles: Ernestine Wade as Sapphire, the Kingfish's nagging wife; Eddie Green as Stonewall, the fast-talking lawyer; Lou Lubin as Shorty, the stuttering barber. They had writers, an orchestra and chorus and guest stars. They jumped back to the top ten and remained there through the '40s. They switched networks, from NBC to CBS, and the show ran from 1948 to 1954 on Sundays. They made $2.5 million after the change.

Then they made the fateful decision to move into television. Gosden and Correll did not think of themselves as bigots. They could not understand the charges that were leveled at them and refused to comment publicly on racial issues. Despite the ill fortune of the television series, the radio format was changed to "The Amos 'n' Andy Music Hall" in which they played DJ's, quipping between records. They did do some skits and the radio show lasted until 1960. Charles J. Correll died in 1972. Freeman F. Gosden remained friends with his long-time partner, and at seventy-nine lives in retirement near Palm Springs, California.

"Amos 'n' Andy" ran head-on into a social revolution— and they lost. Whether stereotypes are in good taste or bad is less a matter of the content than it is the period of time in which you live. At the turn of the century it was acceptable (even encouraged) to stereotype just about anyone. It is presently inappropriate to use ethnic humor of any type *unless* you are a member of the ethnic group that is satirized. "Polish jokes" were frequent in the late sixties and early seventies; now they are not and numerous television series have subsequently emerged that feature characters of Polish descent.

But "Amos 'n' Andy" offended people and went off the air as a result. While they lasted they were a phenomenon. In one sense, Gosden and Correll were one of the most exposed teams that ever existed, reaching a huge listening audience for more than thirty years. In another sense, they were more hidden than the comedy teams of the 1960s and 1970s that were masked by the characters they portrayed. Gosden and Correll were not only white actors playing black roles; they were only heard, never seen except in the very early pre-"Amos 'n' Andy" days. But they were the Caesars of their day and should be recorded in that light.

The Long Road from Peoria to 79 Wistful Vista (Fibber McGee and Molly)

DR. GAMBLE: Hello, Molly. Hello, Neanderthal.

FIBBER: Hiya, Arrowsmith. Kick your case of corn cures into a corner and compose your corpulent corpus on a convenient camp chair.

DR. GAMBLE: Thank's, McGee. Your hospitality is equaled only by your personal beauty. And the prosecution rests.

MOLLY: Had a lot of operations, Doctor? You look tired.

DR. GAMBLE: My dear, I've had more people in stitches today than Bob Hope. But tell me, what's our one-string fiddler doing with the pot-bellied Stradivarius?

FIBBER: This, my ignorant bone-bender, is a mandolin.

   (FIBBER PLAYS)

DR. GAMBLE: McGee, I don't like to be hypercritical, but I've heard prettier music than that from a beer truck running over a manhole cover.

FIBBER: Oh, yeah? And when did you become a music critic, you big fat epidemic chaser?

DR. GAMBLE: Why, you uncultured little faker, I've got more

> music in the first phalanx of my left pinkie than you have in
> your entire family tree.
>
> FIBBER: Don't call me a phalanx, you soggy, sap-headed serum
> salesman!

It doesn't sound that funny, but part of the success of "Fibber McGee and Molly" had to do with the sincerity that Jim and Marian Jordan brought to their roles as Fibber and his long-suffering wife. The Jordans spent ten years trying to make enough money as performers to give up the jobs they both held down to support themselves and their family. When they finally made it they moved slowly but surely up to the number one spot in radio in 1941. As opposed to the sarcasm of Fred Allen or the sketch antics of "Amos 'n' Andy," "Fibber McGee and Molly" was a comedy show that, in hindsight, seems the forerunner of the situation comedy that blanketed early television and is still found all over the tube. There were jokes, with Fibber usually receiving the brunt of the punch lines, but there was an easy, homebody quality to the show that American families identified with and followed fanatically from week to week.

James Edward Jordan was born in 1897 on a farm five miles from Peoria, Illinois. He grew up doing farm chores and singing in the church choir. Marian Driscoll, the daughter of a coalminer, was born in 1898 in Peoria proper and was also a singer. The two met at choir practice at St. John's Church and became childhood sweethearts; he was seventeen at the time, she was sixteen. They both studied music as kids and Marian began teaching the piano before she finished high school. Jim graduated from high school and became a clerk at a wholesale drug outlet before he secured his first professional singing job in 1917 as lead tenor in the vaudeville act "A Night with the Poets." This began a long string of absences from Marian. Not liking life on the road, he returned to his sweetheart and Peoria in 1918, taking up a mail route. They were married in August of that year, but they were not together long.

They did remain married, but five days after the wedding Jim was drafted. He wound up in Paris while Marian held down the fort teaching piano and music in Peoria. The war ended and Jim returned in 1919 to more non-show-business jobs: day laborer, insurance salesman, work in a machine shop, and selling washing machines and vacuum cleaners. He did this until he found out (much like Fibber McGee seemed always to find out) he wasn't going to get any promised commissions on the sales. Marian and Jim continued singing at church and for local clubs in and around Peoria and, after their first child, Kathryn, was born, they got what they thought was their first big break. Their "good fortune" was sixteen weeks on the road as a team. But in order to get the costumes, props, and all the rest they needed for the act they had to sell their car, borrow $500, and lose their home. Their big break used up most of their money, and so they tried another vaudeville tour that lasted until their second child, James, Jr., was born in 1923.

Marian stayed home with the children and Jim struck out for Chicago on his own. He used up most of his money in a few months and, once again, returned home unemployed but determined. Thinking that they would do better as a team and finding life more bearable together, they left the children with relatives and tried one more time. They went broke a few months later in Lincoln, Illinois, about fifty miles from home. They returned defeated, and Marian went back to teaching music while Jim worked in a department store and then a dry-goods store. They sang at lodge halls to supplement their meager income.

The legend is that they got into radio on a bet. In 1925 they were visiting Jim's brother in a Chicago suburb and heard some singers on radio. Jim bet his brother $10 that not only were he and Marian better than the group they heard but that he and his wife could get a job singing on radio. They auditioned for station WJBO and were hired as the "O'Henry Twins." The show lasted five months, but their money worries were not over since they only made $10 for the weekly show.

After the show folded they returned to small-time vaudeville for a while and then got a three times weekly radio show at another station for $60 a week as the "Air Scouts" in 1927. They continued working steadily in radio until they met Don Quinn in 1931. Quinn was an unhappy cartoonist who thought he could make it as a writer in radio. He wrote a series called "Smackout" that NBC put on with Jim and Marian in the leads. Quinn, like Abbott and Costello's writer John Grant, stayed with them and wrote all their shows, adding other writers later when the show became popular. Having a writer was unusual at the time. Comedians usually wrote their own material and it was considered bizarre to use someone else's jokes. But Marian and Jim were not comedians, they were personable singers. The Jordans were the first big-timers to use writers and, of course, the trend was turned upside down in the forties with most comedians doing only other people's material. Hence, a young Dick Martin, later one-half of Rowan and Martin, wrote for another radio hit, "Duffy's Tavern." Comedians did not start writing their own material again until Bob and Ray pioneered the way for the comedy teams of the late fifties and sixties.

The title of the show, "Smackout," referred to Jim's role, a talkative grocer who was "smackout" of everything except hot air. The show ran for four years, being accepted locally in Chicago but never becoming a national hit. In 1935 a new sponsor decided the show should go national; it was retitled "Fibber McGee and Molly" and underwent some changes. Fibber, like the grocer in the first show, told enormous lies and was constantly trying to cover up the un-

*Sincerly McGee
Fibber McGee
+ Molly*

Marian and Jim Jordan ("Fibber McGee and Molly") in the
1950s. (*Courtesy James Jordan*)

truths that he was always caught telling. Besides the obvious limitations of this premise, the show had a corny, homespun style. The first problem was alleviated by alterations; the second was not a problem and was one of the main factors in the show's eventual popularity. Over the next few years the format of the show was directed toward making Fibber's and Molly's characters more the "little man with big talk and ideas" and his patient, yet petulant wife. The show was polished and new characters, like Dr. Gamble, Mrs. Uppington, and Myrt, the telephone operator who was never heard by the listening audience (she was just responded to via the telephone). A similar type of device has recently been used on television in the "Rhoda" series starring Valerie Harper. Carleton, the usually tippling doorman (played by writer/producer Lorenzo Music), is never seen on the tube, only heard through the intercom. But with all of the changes "Fibber McGee and Molly" went through, Fibber always retained some of his tall-storytelling ability.

By the 1940s the McGees had moved to their famous address at 79 Wistful Vista and were a nationwide success. Fibber was usually well intentioned and incompetent; Molly was always understanding, if tart, with Fibber's blustering ways. But when she put her foot down, Fibber listened, setting a pattern for all the later television situation comedies. Father does not always know best, usually Mother does. The show was sentimental in many ways, but that's what the public loved. Marian played Molly and the nerve-shattering Teeny, the young girl next door who drove Fibber up a wall consistently with questions like, "Whatcha' doin,' huh, mister, whatcha'?" Another character on the show, the pompous deep-throated Throckmorton P. Gildersleeve (played by Harold Peary), became so popular that he eventually "moved away" from the McGees and got his own show, "The Great Gildersleeve." That series went over to television later with first Jackie Gleason, then William Bendix in the lead, faring much better than Jim and Marian's jump to television.

The Jordans tried to expand their careers and did their first film with Betty Grable and Jackie Coogan for Paramount in 1938 (*This Way, Please*). They did not become stars from the exposure but later signed to do a film a year for RKO Radio Pictures, including *Here We Go Again* with Edgar Bergen and Charlie McCarthy, *Look Who's Laughing*, again with Bergen and McCarthy and adding Lucille Ball, and, in 1944, *Heavenly Days*. Pleasant though they were, Jim and Marian did not make a name in films.

By 1941 "Fibber McGee and Molly" was at the top of radio, making $3,500 a week for its stars and beating names like Jack Benny and Bob Hope, not to mention "Amos 'n' Andy," into first place in the ratings. The show lasted in a half-hour version until 1953, switching then to fifteen minutes, five days a week until 1957. In the late 1950s Jim and Marian preceded the later stint of Bob and Ray on NBC's "Monitor" radio show doing five-minute spots.

Characters on the show came and went, as did actors during World War II. Gale Gordon, who later played second banana to Lucille Ball in her last two television series, was Mayor La Trivia and Foggy Williams. Bill Thompson played Wallace Wimple, Horatio K. Boomer, who could outhustle W. C. Fields, the Old Timer, and Nick the Greek (not the Las Vegas gambler). Beulah, the Black maid, was played by a white man, Marlin Hurt. (Beulah got her own show too.)

When they tried to move "Fibber" and cast to television, it just did not work out. The blame has been attributed to the writers, but there is no definite answer. In 1959 another version of "Fibber McGee and Molly" was done on NBC with Bob Sweeney and Cathy Lewis taking on the lead roles, but this show did not go either. Marian Jordan was ill in the late fifties and died in 1961. Jim Jordan, now seventy-eight, lives in retirement in Beverly Hills.

"Fibber McGee and Molly" superseded "Amos 'n' Andy" as America's favorite show. Fibber's famous closet, containing more paraphernalia than an inventor's garage and showering Fibber with odds and ends whenever he forgot and opened it, kept people's interest for twenty years. To vary the gleeful expectation, sometimes everything didn't fall on Fibber, but the audience always awaited whatever the outcome and laughed. The show was perhaps the most wholesome show on radio, even preaching at times.

Jim and Marian were one of three married teams who made it big in show business as comedy teams. They are from the same era as Burns and Allen, while Stiller and Meara are a team of the sixties and seventies. The Jordans' long struggle to make it from one-night stands and singing for a few dollars at the lodge to one of the nation's most loved comedy teams is a study in tenacity. They wanted success badly enough and worked hard and long to get it.

Slapstock, Slapstuck, and Slapstick (The Three Stooges)

STOOGE (stōōj), n., v., stooged, stooging, -n. l. Informal. an entertainer who feeds lines to the main comedian and usually serves as the butt of his jokes.

Most comedians had stooges in vaudeville. It took some time for a stooge to work up to straight man, a much more dignified role. The roles of the funny man and the straight man evolved so that the comic embodied many of the stooge's qualities, while the straight man took on some of the comic's attributes. Stooges, at first, always got the dirty end of the stick. Lou Costello was not Bud Abbott's stooge—he was the comic, Abbott the straight man. But Abbott was always pummeling Costello, slapping his face or pulling him along by the tie. It was a technique that had become a part of burlesque, and Bud and Lou had started in burlesque; but the roughhouse had definite elements of slap-stick.

Slapstick is not listed in the *Oxford English Dictionary*, but the word derives from a wooden paddle. The flat end of the paddle was composed of two separate pieces that hit together, making a loud noise, when the paddle came in contact with another object. It may have been used earlier, but the slap stick was definitely used in the sixteenth century by performers in the *commedia dell'arte*. This was Italian popular comedy (as mentioned earlier) in which masked entertainers improvised from a plot outline that had stock situations and involved stock characters. The actors carried the slap sticks in the sash around their waists and when a scalliwag did or said something unseemly, he would be whacked loudly. The noise sounded as if he were really being hit very hard. The *commedia dell'arte* gave rise to slapstick as well as to the improvisational techniques used by the comics in the late 1950s and to the present. The technique was usually used by a team rather than a single comedian. But these two traditions take opposite ends of the pole.

Improvisation at its most sophisticated is represented by Mike Nichols and Elaine May. The Three Stooges were opposed to anything that made sense and did not involve a fall. Nobody received more physical abuse than the Three Stooges. They took slapstick to its furthest extreme, inflicting all manner of mayhem on themselves and others. They slapped, slugged, tripped, kicked, head-butted, stepped-on, poked, prodded, pulled, dunked, doused, dropped, spritzed, spit water in the face, threw pies in the schnozz, pinched cheeks, and used any form of liquid and/or solid to sully each other. Their dialogue consisted of simple vaudeville or burlesque jokes that led to another battering. An example from the short *Studio Stoops:*

SHEMP: When I come back I'll give you the password.
MOE: What'll it be?
SHEMP: Open the door. *(Moe slaps Shemp.)*

Samuel (Shemp) Howard was born in 1901, Moe Howard in 1905, and Jerry (Curly) Howard in 1911 in Brooklyn, New York. Moe ran away from the rigors of school in Bensonhurst, Brooklyn, at nine and began playing the riverboat circuit on the Mississippi. He moved up to traveling theatrical troupes performing in the gamut of styles from Shakespeare to "Ten Nights in a Bar Room." He and Shemp teamed up as a blackface team after the fashion of Moran and Mack. Smith and Dale had done a blackface turn in their early days, too. Shemp and Moe had an acrobatic background that, like Smith and Dale, seemed almost a necessity for being a vaudeville comedian. Moe replaced an acrobat in Ted Healy's vaudeville act in 1922, bringing Shemp along with him. They stayed with Healy for ten years.

Laurence (Larry) Fine was born in Philadelphia in 1911. He started out to be an actor, as did the Howard brothers, and joined the two brothers with Healy in 1928 after many comedic exploits including the sissy role in the often seen high school bit and an act called the Haney Sisters and Fine. Joe Besser, who was later one of the team, played a similar sissy on Abbott and Costello's television series; Besser played the role of Stinky on Bud and Lou's series, usually threatening Lou with an oversized lollipop and whining, "I'll harm you." The high school routine had many variations, running from the Gus Edwards' original to the Marx Brothers "Fun in Hi Skule" and Smith and Dale's school act "The New Teacher."

While Moe and Shemp were touring "A Night in Venice" with Healy, they came across a violinist playing in a Chicago cafe. The way Larry Fine performed convinced Healy to add him as one of his stooges. The billing of the act had changed by then to "Ted Healy and His Stooges." Besides tours and vaudeville, they did Broadway revues like *Earl Carroll's Vanities* in the late 1920s. As vaudevillians gravitated to the rich field of movies, Healy made *Soup to Nuts*, written by Rube Goldberg, for Fox in 1930. He brought Moe, Larry, and Shemp with him to make the feature length film, but they were billed as his "racketeers" not his stooges.

After their cinematic debut, the troupe returned to vaudeville and revues like *The Passing Show of 1932*. Their next film, bringing them to Hollywood again, was *Dancing Ladies*, starring Joan Crawford and Clark Gable, for MGM in 1933, Shemp had gone off on his own to make a film, so he was replaced with the youngest Howard brother, Curly. Curly had been doing comedy for a while, his last assignment being the comedy conductor for Orville Knapp's orchestra. He shaved his head and his mustache to make it as one of Healy's stooges. The group did a number of shorts and a few features for MGM; they even managed to fit in some club work in Los Angeles at the Club New Yorker.

Moe, Larry, and Curly decided to go it on their own and starred in their first short for Columbia in 1933 (*Woman Haters*). They stayed with Columbia, outlasting all the other contract players, for twenty-five years. During that time they made over 190 shorts and a number of features. In *Woman Haters* they did not appear as a team but as three separate characters. Their next short found them billed as Howard, Fine, and Howard. The third one, although panned by the critics, really got them started as a team. *Men in Black*, a send-up of a hit film at the time, put them on the show-business map and was their only effort to be nominated for an Academy Award. They then went next to a series of hospital satires, a form that a group of British actors used to good effect in the sixties with the *Carry On* pictures.

The original Three Stooges (Larry Fine, l.; Curly Howard, m.; Moe Howard, r.) in "Goofs and Saddles," a 1937 short. (*Courtesy Norman Maurer*)

The Three Stooges worked with a lot of directors, including Charlie Chase and Del Lord, one of the original Keystone Kops for Mack Sennett. Like Smith and Dale and, later, Abbott and Costello, the Three Stooges were never appreciated by the critics because they used corny, slapstick material. The jokes kept cropping up over and over and the two-reel shorts were episodic, using the same material—the later films borrowed clips freely from their earlier films. They were also accused of being too violent. Every Stooges' film is a study in physical endurance for the three. But their major audience, the kids, did not think it was too violent. In their later years, the Stooges were the last holdover from silent films, with physical action being the end-all of their act.

In 1946 Curly had a stroke and he dropped out of the group. He died a few years later in 1952 at the young age of forty-one. His older brother, Shemp, rejoined the Stooges after working in many films on his own. The level of the shorts, never the caliber of Cecil B. DeMille, began dropping off even more in the late forties, particularly after Curly left. Shemp was good but he wasn't Curly. Different gambits were attempted to punch up the films, including a dismal foray into three-dimensional movies in 1952.

In 1956 Shemp died, also at a young age (fifty-one). He was replaced by Joe Besser, who was Stinky on Abbott and Costello's TV show and is now heard on many children's cartoon shows as the voice of various characters. The shorts were done with even more haste and less taste in the fifties

The Three Stooges (with Shemp Howard replacing Curly) doing one of their numerous pie-in-the-face bits in one of 200 shorts, "Bedlam In Paradise" (1956). (Larry, l.; Shemp, m.; Moe, r.) (*Courtesy Norman Maurer*)

and do not match up with the earlier efforts of Moe, Larry, and Curly. In 1957 Columbia let the Stooges' contract run out, retaining enough unreleased film to keep showing "new" shorts through 1959. Unemployed, the Stooges decided to do a personal appearance tour but Besser dropped out, not wanting to leave his wife for the loneliness of the road. Moe did a solo in the film *Space Master X-7*, one of the all-time greats after *2,000,000 B.C.*, and reruns of "The Gong Show."

It looked as if the act was finally over when Screen Gems, the television arm of Columbia, reissued some of the old shorts to television in 1958. As with other film teams—Laurel and Hardy, the Marx Four, Abbott and Costello—the Stooges were due for rediscovery by new generations. There was such a good reaction, especially from children, that they had an unprecedented 150-plus stations pick up the shorts. This led to nightclub bookings and TV guest shots. Joe De Rita, a veteran nightclub, radio, and film comedian replaced Besser and was nicknamed Curly Joe. Columbia took the hint from TV and began filming a feature starring the revitalized Three Stooges. They made *Have Rocket Will Travel* in 1959 and made four more features through 1963. They joined others in two 1963 films in which they shared billing: *It's a Mad Mad Mad Mad World* for Stanley Kramer at United Artists and *Four for Texas* at Warners. *Stop! Look! and Laugh!* was a reissue in 1961 of a number of older shorts with a narrator linking the action together.

After another gap, they started doing their own voices in a series of Three Stooges cartoons, completing over 150 in all. In the sixties, with the renewed interest in them, they guested on Joey Bishop's talk show as the Ritz Brothers did, and with Steve Allen and Ed Sullivan. Then their appearances became infrequent and stopped. Larry Fine had been with the act longer than anyone except Moe Howard, the head stooge with the bangs covering his forehead. Larry went into retirement and died a few months before Moe in 1975. Joe De Rita was the last man to join the Stooges and has not performed regularly since the act broke up. Moe Howard had started the act back in 1922 with Healy. He made it all hang together, trying to shape the other two up while bumbling miserably himself. Moe died at seventy in 1975.

The Three Stooges were, like silent film stars, almost purely visual in their act. It is obvious that they were not going to make it in radio. But they remained slapstick at its best and at its worst. They have the same appeal for the young as Road Runner cartoons. We all know that the weird-looking little bird is going to be triumphant and that the evil predator, the slick coyote, will be knocked silly while trying to catch the road runner. This similarity to cartoons is probably why the Stooges are seen every week as animated robots on Saturday morning. They lend themselves easily to the mechanized, two-dimensional world of comics and cartoons. The Three Stooges were three banged-about coyotes who are always going to mess everything up and then hit each other.

They made almost twenty-five features and nearly two hundred shorts, not counting the work they did on their own. And the shorts are still running every week across the nation. The team was together, in one combination or another, from 1923 until the early 1970s—over forty years. If their dialogue is wooden or silly, if their constant hitting and falling gets tedious, taken in small doses the Three Stooges will make almost anyone laugh. And the younger audiences think they are the best.

Comedy is simply making people laugh. But comedians, being human, want to make people laugh *and* be stars, headliners, in the big time. A few want to change society. A book about comedians or comedy teams cannot hope to compete, nor should it try to compete, with the people who do it best. Such a book should try to inform and entertain. It is hoped the flavor of the comedy comes through.

From 1898, when Smith and Dale formed a comedy team, until the 1978 release of Cheech and Chong's first feature film, is eighty years. The laughs that are recorded continue; those that are not are remembered. The best of comedy lives on in the comedians who are still alive.

There is no end to comedy. The following exchange is between the late Margaret Dumont (as Mrs. Teasdale) and the late and immortal Groucho Marx (as Rufus T. Firefly) in *Duck Soup*:

FIREFLY: . . . Not that I care, but where is your husband?
TEASDALE: Why, he's dead.
FIREFLY: I'll bet he's just using that as an excuse.

Glossary

The majority of terms that may not be familiar to the reader have been explained in the text. But in case there is any confusion, the following definitions should clear things up. This is not meant as a thorough glossary of show-business slang, but merely as a helpful guide to this book.

Ad Lib—Varying a line, or throwing in a totally new line, in a set routine or script.

Banana, Top—The top banana was the lead comic in vaudeville and remains the designation of the featured comedian. The second banana took a secondary role to the top banana.

Big Time/Small Time—There were two kinds of vaudeville: big time meant you only did two shows a day and were doing all right; small time required up to six shows a day.

Billing—The order of the acts in vaudeville. Top of the bill meant you were featured; bottom of the bill meant you were the dogs. *But,* opening the show was the worst spot in the show, closing the show was the best. So, if you were at the top of the bill, you closed the show.

Bit—This is a short piece of comedy business. It could be physical business, "the pie in the face" bit or it could be a short routine, "Who's on First."

Blocking—Where the director tells you to go and when he tells you to go there. It includes entrances, exits, and all moves during the scene.

Boffo B.O. Biz—Show-business slang for really good (boffo) box office (b.o.) receipts (biz). Biz, as in show biz, is short for business.

Borscht Belt (Circuit)—Hotels and cafes in the Catskill Mountains (upper New York) that are known as a series of spots that comedians and other entertainers play when they are breaking into the business. The Borscht Belt still exists but frequently books name acts.

Business—Anything that is done that is not part of the script or bit. Also, any minor activity that is not a part of the whole. After you have slipped on the banana peel and investigated what made you slip, folding up the peel and putting it in your pocket is a piece of business.

Burlesque (Burlie, Burleque)—A form of live entertainment on a stage that involved minimally clad women, musical numbers and risqué humor. It was an offshoot of vaudeville.

Cliff Hanger—An ending that is not resolved, leading you to have a great deal of concern about the outcome of the proceedings. Used in early film serials and radio a great deal. At the end of the show the heroine is tied to the railroad tracks and . . .

Dialect Humor—A comic use of the various dialects immigrants brought to America. It was in vogue at the turn of the century, then began to diminish in the 1950s. There still are dialect comedians (Myron Cohen). The most prevalent were German (Weber and Fields), Italian (Chico Marx as Ravelli), Dutch (Lou Costello's first job as a comic), Jewish (Groucho), Irish (Gracie Allen before she joined George), and Black (Amos 'n' Andy).

Eccentric Dancing—A form of informal dancing that took tap dancing or soft-shoe dancing and treated it comedically. The dancer would do bizarre-looking steps like Ray Bolger in *The Wizard of Oz*.

Emcee—An emcee acted as a master of ceremonies, introducing acts and usually making jokes. Most burlesque comics were emcees.

Emmy—The highest award given in television.

English Music Hall—A form of variety entertainment in England that preceded and was similar to vaudeville. It involved musical numbers, comedy, mime, and various novelty acts such as jugglers and trained seals. It was a major influence on both American vaudeville and American musical comedy.

Extra—Nonspeaking roles in films. In early films extras were called supers, short for supernumeraries. Now they are called extras or "atmosphere."

Feature—A full-length film, as opposed to shorts which averaged ten minutes and went for one or two reels of film.

Fourth Wall—An imaginary wall created by the performer that separates that performer from the audience. Used as an acting technique to facilitate concentration.

Fright Wig—A wig that was extreme in one way or another. It was used as a comedic device and was so outrageous that it appeared as if the wearer were frightened to death.

Gag—A joke. A gag might be put into a routine that needs some beefing up (help). **Gag Man**—A writer for comedians. **Running Gag**—A joke that is mentioned once and then is referred to again. The references to the same joke are supposed to get more laughs each time it is mentioned. A running gag usually does not occur more than three or four times in a routine or a play/film/TV show. Neil Simon, the comedy writer, is a master of the running gag.

Gig—A job in show business. The term was originally a musician's term.

Headliner—Someone at the top of the bill; the featured act.

Heavy—The bad guy. Villains wore heavy make-up in silent films: bushy eyebrows, mustaches, beards. The term evolved from this use.

Hiatus—The period when a TV series is done shooting for a season and has not begun shooting for the next season. Usually from the end of March or beginning of April until July or August.

Hoofer—Slang for a professional dancer. It originated in vaudeville and really refers to someone who did tap and/or soft shoe. Quite often the dancer picked up the craft with little or no lessons.

Improv, Improvisation—An extended form of ad-libbing. With roots in the sixteenth-century art of *commedia dell'arte,* a form of theater in Italy, improvisation was used as a technique to study acting by the great Russian teacher Stanislavski. In an improv, which is short for improvisation, one is given a character and a goal and then must improvise a scene without a script.

Ingenue—A naive, young girl. Ingenue became a type of role. The male counterpart is the **Juvenile.**

In the Can—The film is shot, so the celluloid reverts to the metal can it is kept in.

Laugh Track—A recording of laughter used on some comedy television shows.

Limelight—Originally the means of illuminating the front of the stage, or apron, by gas, rather than electricity. It has come to mean being in the spotlight, limelight being the early form of spotlighting a performer. Also, anyone who is well known.

Lip-Synch (Lip Synchronization, Dumb Act)—Mouthing the words to recorded material. A prevalent act in vaudeville. Jerry Lewis used this kind of act to break into the business.

Master Shot—In film and early TV, the shot that included all of the action. Close-ups were shot later.

Matinee Idol—A leading man whom women idolized. The term derives from early films and matinee (afternoon) audiences.

Medium (pl. Media)—This has come to mean the various instruments of communication: film, TV, newspapers, etc.

Mime (Pantomime)—Both imply silent acting-out of a character and that character's experiences. Mime was instrumental in silent films.

Monologue (Monologist)—One person talking to a group or, in literature, to the world. A monologist is one who gives a monologue. In comedy, it was the beginning of the single stand-up comic. The monologue was usually an extended story, as opposed to the present-day stand-up comic who gives a series of views and jokes about many subjects and themes.

Obie—Award for an Off-Broadway production of a play in any of the fields: actor, writer, director, designer, lyricist, etc.

Olio—Originally an act performed downstage while the upstage was being reset for the next performer. It came to mean the curtain that covered the upstage activity from the audience.

One Nighter (One-Night Stand)—Usually a series of live performances that play only one night in each town. Also, X-rated.

One Reeler (Two Reeler)—The early films that were very short and consisted of one (or two) reels of film.

On the Halls—British music hall term for performing, getting it before the audience. American theatrical slang uses on the boards.

Oscar—The highest award the film industry gives.

Outtake—In a film or a filmed TV show, it takes a number of times to get a scene the way the director wants it. Each of these recordings of the scene on film is called a take. Outtakes are the takes not used and, in a comedy, usually are records of some pretty funny mistakes. Even in dramas they can be hilarious.

Payoff—The laughter that comes after a joke is successful. If the joke is not successful, there is no payoff. If most of the jokes are unsuccessful, there may not be any pay.

Physical Humor—Comedy that does not require words: a pie in the face, a fall from slipping on a banana peel.

Playing the Palace—The height of vaudeville. The Palace Theater was the equivalent of getting an Oscar, Emmy, Tony, or Obie.

Prop—From the word *property*. On a film the prop person handles all of the things one uses in a scene: a gun, a pen, a duck, a car. Comedy props were used to get laughs, so a part of your wardrobe could become a prop (Stan's and Ollie's hats). Groucho's cigar was a prop as is George Burns's stogie; Harpo's horn was a prop; the phone used by Nichols and May was a prop.

Punch Line—In a comedy sequence of lines, the line that is supposed to get the laugh. Abbott and Costello: Bud: "To get in the house you must go through escrow." Lou: "Why can't I go through Glendale." Lou has the punch line.

Red Sluggers—Whiskers used in vaudeville.

Revue—A stage combination of skits, songs, and dances. It has later come to mean the above with an eye to parody.

Roast—A comedy format borrowed from the Friars' Club in which a celebrity is honored by friends. The "honor" involves the friends, usually fellow comedians, who do nine minutes of comedy insults and one minute of praise.

Routine—An individual, set piece of (comedy) material.

Segment—One show in a series, or one portion of one show.

Sequel—In films, another film that continues the action and characters of the original picture. Abbott and Costello's *Buck Privates Come Home* was a sequel to *Buck Privates*, their first starring film.

Short—An early film that lasted about ten minutes and consisted of one reel. Later included slightly longer films of two reels.

Shtick—A Yiddish term for comedy business.

Sight Gag—A nonverbal joke. Olsen and Johnson, the early vaudeville team, did a bit that had Johnson shoot a gun into the air and a chicken would fall to the stage. Olsen said: "It's a good thing that cows don't fly." Johnson shot the gun again and a cow fell on the stage. Laurel and Hardy and the Marx Brothers were masters of sight gags.

Situation Comedy—A premise that has the same situation, although varied, on each show. "I Love Lucy" and "The Mary Tyler Moore Show" were situation comedies.

Sketch—A short comedy routine that has the comedians play-

Glossary 221

ing roles in a set situation: Smith and Dale's "Dr. Kronkhite" is a sketch.

Skit—The same as a sketch, sometimes shorter.

Slow Burn—A kind of comedy take; reacting to something in anger, but in a slow, controlled anger that usually precedes an emotional explosion, if not a physical one.

Soap—Short for soap opera; an ongoing story, usually melo-dramatic and sentimental, that exposes the ups and downs of a large cast of characters. The name derives from the early sponsors of radio operas; their product was soap.

Song-and-Dance Man—Very simply, a person in vaudeville who sang and danced, interlacing his dancing with occasional jokes, particularly in a team. George Burns was originally a song-and-dance man.

Sound Stage—Huge enclosed buildings, three or four stories high, with no windows, in which movies and TV shows are filmed.

SRO—Show business slang for good business: standing room only.

Stand-up Routine (Comic)—A stand-up routine meant, simply, that there was no other act on stage and that you were standing up, doing a talking act. Abbott and Costello did stand-up routines in burlesque. A stand-up comic was originally a monologist and is now any comic who works alone and tells jokes. A stand-up routine could be done by a monologist or a team.

Stock Player—Someone under contract to a studio and part of their stable of performers, as opposed to someone who does sum-mer stock.

Straight Man—The straight man set up the jokes, the comic did the jokes. He also kept the comic from getting too far away from the premise if the comic ad-libbed or improvised. In later teams these roles became interchangeable, but usually the person ask-ing the question was playing straight at the moment. "Who was that lady I saw you with last night?" "That was no lady, that was my wife."

Subplot—A plot other than the main plot, that weaves in and out of the story line. In the Marx Brothers' films, the young lovers and their troubles became the major subplot.

Summer Stock—Plays given in the summer that last for six to eight weeks, usually hitting one town a week. Alaska is not a big summer stock state.

Take—A reaction, usually comedic, to something that is done.

When Stan Laurel did something dumb and Ollie looked straight at the camera in disgust, that was a take. The slow burn is a classic take used in silent films and still going strong.

Talkies—Pictures with sound; the slang term for talking pictures.

Talking Act—A comedy act that did not involve dancing, singing, juggling, magic, mime.

Talking Woman—The female equivalent of a straight man.

Trailer—The short footage that previews a feature film in order to build up interest. It is usually known as "previews of coming attractions."

Turkey—A flop.

Vaudeville—The later, American version of English music hall that involved a series of acts including comedy routines, singing, dancing, juggling, acrobatics, magic, mime, and cockatoos-seals-dogs, etc. Vaudeville began in the late eighteenth century and died in the early 1930s. There are occasional revivals, some of them now seen on television.

Chronology

SMITH AND DALE

1880s

1881   —Charles Marks (CHARLIE DALE) born in New York City

1884   —Joe Sultzer (JOE SMITH) born in New York City

1890s

1898   —first performance as a team as Marks and Sultzer

1900s

1900   —become the Avon Comedy Four with two supporting performers, playing vaudeville and burlesque

1902–14—famous "school act," "The New Teacher"

1906   —win test case against New York City "blue laws." Result: Sunday performances permitted in New York City for first time

1909   —tour of Ireland, England, Scotland, Wales

1910s

1914   —headline first all-American bill in London

1916   —Broadway debut in *Why Worry?* with Fanny Brice

1916   —make short comedy phonograph recordings for Victor label

1919   —first known as Smith and Dale

1920s

1920–30—many vaudeville performances and benefit shows

1929   —film "shorts" for Paramount and Warner Brothers

1929   —headline at the Palladium in London

1930s

1931   —Broadway play, *Mendel, Inc.*
1932   —feature film *The Heart of New York*
1933–39—Broadway and numerous radio appearances
1939   —film comedy shorts, *A Nag in the Bag* and *Mutiny on the Body*

1940s

1948   —50th anniversary as a team—honored by the Lambs' Club, New York

1950s

1950–60—frequent TV appearances on "The Ed Sullivan Show"
1951   —feature film *Two Tickets to Broadway*
1952   —appear at the Palace Theater with Judy Garland

1960s

1968   —final performance as a team, the Lambs' Club, New York

1970s

1971   —Charlie Dale dies, New Jersey
1972   —*The Sunshine Boys,* a comedy by Neil Simon based on the lives of Smith and Dale opens on Broadway
1978   —Joe Smith alive and well in New Jersey

THE MARX BROTHERS

1880s

1887   —Leonard (CHICO) Marx born in New York City
1888   —Arthur (HARPO) Marx born in New York City

1890s

1890   —Julius (GROUCHO) Marx born in New York City
1897   —Milton (GUMMO) Marx born in New York City

1900s

1901   —Herbert (ZEPPO) Marx born in New York City

1910s

——————

1920s

1925 —Broadway play, *The Cocoanuts*
1928 —Broadway play, *Animal Crackers*
1929 —first feature film, *The Cocoanuts* (see separate listing for complete record of Marx Brothers films)

1930s

1933 —feature film, *Duck Soup,* marks last film appearance of Zeppo and the beginning of the team of three, Groucho, Harpo, Chico.

1940s

1947 —radio premiere of Groucho's quiz show, "You Bet Your Life"
1948 —"You Bet Your Life" awarded Peabody Award for excellence in radio
1949 —feature film, *Love Happy,* last film as a team

1950s

1950–61—"You Bet Your Life" becomes a top television show
1959 —television, "The Incredible Jewel Robbery," last appearance in public as a team

1960s

1961 —Chico Marx dies
1962 —new, short-lived television show, "Tell It to Groucho"
1962–65—television show, "The Best of Groucho"
1964 —Harpo Marx dies

1970s

1972 —Cannes Film Festival Award commemorating the contribution of the Marx Brothers to world cinema
1977 —Gummo Marx dies in May; Groucho Marx dies in August
1978 —Zeppo Marx living in retirement on the West Coast

LAUREL AND HARDY

1880s

1890s

1890   —Arthur Stanley Jefferson (STAN LAUREL) born in England
1892   —OLIVER Norvell ("Babe") HARDY born in Georgia

1900s

1909(?)—Stan Laurel is understudy to Charlie Chaplin in British mime show

1910s

1910   —Stan Laurel, American stage debut in British music hall show
1913   —Oliver Hardy film debut in *Outwitting Dad*
1917   —Stan Laurel film debut in *Nuts in May*
1918   —appear separately in same film, *Lucky Dog*

1920s

1926   —appear together in silent film short, *Slipping Wives*
1926   —first Laurel and Hardy film, silent short, *Putting Pants on Philip*—official debut as a team (see separate listing for complete record of Laurel and Hardy feature films and selected short films)

1930s

1930   —nation's top comedy stars
1930   —first Laurel and Hardy sound film, *Unaccustomed as We Are*
1931   —first feature film, *Pardon Us*
1932   —only Academy Award winning film, *The Music Box,* a film short

1940s

1940   —The Laurel and Hardy Revue—a live touring show in the U.S.A.
1947   —tour of England, Sweden, Denmark, Belgium, France

1950s

1950–52—last film, *Atoll K* (also released as *Utopia*)
1952   —tour of England
1955   —films released to television
1957   —Oliver Hardy dies in Los Angeles

1960s

1964   —Stan Laurel dies in Santa Monica, California

1970s

————

AMOS 'N' ANDY

1880s

————

1890s

1890   —Charles J. Correll (ANDY) born in Peoria, Illinois
1899   —Freeman F. Gosden (AMOS) born in Richmond, Virginia

1900s

————

1910s

————

1920s

1925   —WGN radio—song and joke act
1926   —"Sam 'n' Henry Show"—local radio
1928   —"Amos 'n' Andy" premieres on local radio
1929   —"Amos 'n' Andy" premieres on NBC network radio— fifteen minute show daily

1930s

1937   —"Amos 'n' Andy moves to the West Coast—thirty minute show

1940s

1940–50—"Amos 'n' Andy" continues as most popular radio show

1950s

1954   —final radio appearance of "Amos 'n' Andy"
1954   —"The Amos 'n' Andy Music Hall" debuts on CBS radio—
          records, skits, jokes

1960s

1960   —last performance of "The Amos 'n' Andy Music Hall"

1970s
1972   —Charles J. Correll dies
1978   —Freeman F. Gosden alive and well in southern California

ABBOTT AND COSTELLO

1880s

———

1890s

1895   —William (BUD) ABBOTT born in Asbury Park, New
          Jersey

1900s

1906   —Louis Francis Cristillo (LOU COSTELLO) born in
          Paterson, New Jersey

1910s

———

1920s

———

1930s
1936   —work together and officially become a team in New
          York City
1939   —only Broadway play, *The Streets of Paris*

1940s

1940   —first film, *One Night in the Tropics*
1941   —national radio show, "Abbott and Costello"
1941   —first starring film, *Buck Privates* (see separate listing for complete record of Abbott and Costello films)

1950s

1951   —television debut on "The Colgate Comedy Hour"
1952   —television, "The Abbott and Costello Show"
1956   —last film as a team, *Dance with Me Henry*
1957   —team dissolves
1959   —Costello film alone, *The Thirty-Foot Bride of Candy Rock*
1959   —Lou Costello dies in Los Angeles

1960s

1960–70—films released to television

1970s

1974   —Bud Abbott dies in Los Angeles
1976   —Saturday television cartoon series, "Abbott and Costello"

BURNS AND ALLEN

1880s

———

1890s

1896   —Nathan Birnbaum (GEORGE BURNS) born in New York City

1900s

1906   —Gracie Ethel Cecile Rosalie Allen born in San Francisco

1910s

———

1920s

1922   —debut as a team, Philadelphia
1926   —married in Cleveland, Ohio
1929   —first film (short), *Lambchops* (see separate listing for complete record of Burns and Allen films)

1930s

1930   —first radio appearance—British Broadcasting Corporation, London, England
1932   —CBS Radio debut of "The Burns and Allen Show"
1932   —first feature film, *The Big Broadcast*
1939   —last film as a team, *Honolulu*

1940s

1940–49—radio show continues
1940   —Gracie runs for President as the candidate of the Surprise Party
1949   —appearance at the Palladium in London

1950s

1950   —Television debut of "The George Burns and Gracie Allen Show," replaces radio show
1958   —June 4, final television show, Gracie retires

1960s

1964   —Gracie Allen dies in Los Angeles

1970s

1975   —George Burns wins Oscar as Best Supporting Actor in the film version of *The Sunshine Boys*
1978   —George Burns stars as God in the film *Oh, God* directed by Carl Reiner
1978   —George stars in film, *Sergeant Pepper's Lonely Hearts Club Band*
1978   —television special, "George Burns' 100th Birthday Party"

FIBBER MCGEE AND MOLLY

1880s

1890s

1897   —James Edward Jordan (FIBBER McGEE) born in Peoria, Illinois

1898   —Marian Driscoll (MOLLY) born in Peoria, Illinois

1900s

1910s

1918   —Jim Jordan and Marian Driscoll marry in Illinois

1920s

1925   —work as radio singers known as "The O'Henry Twins"

1920–30—tour U.S.A. as singers

1930s

1931   —first radio series, "Smackout"

1935   —national radio debut of "Fibber McGee and Molly" show

1938   —first film, *This Way Please*

1940s

1941   —"Fibber McGee and Molly" is #1 radio show in nation

1941   —second film, *Look Who's Laughing*

1942   —third film, *Here We Go Again*

1944   —final film, *Heavenly Days*

1950s

1956   —final year of "Fibber McGee and Molly" radio show

1956–59—series of five-minutes comedy spots for "Monitor," NBC radio

1960s

1961   —Marian Jordan dies

1978   —Jim Jordan living in retirement, Beverly Hills, California

THE THREE STOOGES

1880s

1890s

1900s

1901   —Samuel Howard (SHEMP) born in New York City
1905   —Moe Howard (MOE) born in New York City

1910s

1911   —Jerry Howard (CURLY) born in Brooklyn, New York
1911   —Laurence Fine (LARRY) born in Philadelphia, Pennsylvania

1920s

1920(?)—Moe and Shemp do a blackface vaudeville act
1923   —Moe and Shemp team with Ted Healy in vaudeville for Ted Healy and His Stooges
1928   —Larry Fine joins them in Healy's act

1930s

1930   —first film (with Healy), *Soup to Nuts*
1931–33—vaudeville with Healy
1934   —first short film as the Three Stooges, *Men in Black* (see separate listing for complete record of Three Stooges feature films)
1934–58—made over 200 film shorts

1940s

1950s

1952   —Curly Howard dies
1956   —Shemp Howard dies
1956   —Joe Besser replaces Shemp in films
1958   —Stooges films packaged for television

1960s

1965 —Stooges cartoons made and released to television
1965 —last film, *The Outlaws Is Coming*

1970s

1975 —Moe Howard dies
1975 —Larry Fine dies

MARTIN AND LEWIS

1880s

1890s

1900s

1910s

1917 —Dino Paul Crocetti (DEAN MARTIN) born in Steubenville, Ohio

1920s

1926 —Joseph Levitch (JERRY LEWIS) born in Newark, New Jersey

1930s

1940s

1946 —first appearance as a team, New Jersey
1949 —first film, *My Friend Irma* (see separate listing for complete record of Martin and Lewis films)
1949–52—radio, "Martin and Lewis Show"

1950s

1950   —television, "Texaco Star Theatre" and "Colgate Comedy
             Hour"
1950/51—voted #1 box office draw in nation
1956   —last film, *Hollywood or Bust*
1956   —last appearance as a team, the Copacabana, New York

1960s

1960–78—Dean Martin—variety of film roles including Matt Helm;
             television appearances including 'The Dean Martin
             Show" (in various forms, 1965–77); occasional Las
             Vegas performances
1960–78—Jerry Lewis—actor, director, producer of numerous film
             comedies; occasional work in nightclubs; television
             guest appearances; annual muscular dystrophy telethon

REINER AND BROOKS

1920s

1922   —Carl Reiner born in the Bronx, New York
1926(?)—Melvyn Kaminsky (MEL BROOKS) born in Brooklyn,
             New York

1930s

———

1940s

———

1950s

1950   —meet on Sid Caesar's "Your Show of Shows"

1960s

1960   —first album, "2,000 Years with Carl Reiner and Mel
             Brooks"
1962   —second album, "2,001 Years with Reiner and Brooks"
1963   —third album, "Reiner and Brooks at the Cannes Film
             Festival"

1940s

1973   —fourth album, "2,000 and Thirteen"
1978   —Reiner film, *Oh, God* stars George Burns
1978   —Brooks film, *High Anxiety*

The Individual Work of Carl Reiner and Mel Brooks

CARL REINER

1957   —Emmy for Best Supporting Actor, "Your Show of Shows"
1958   —published novel, *Enter Laughing* (later a film starring Elaine May)
1959   —writer for "The Dinah Shore Show"
1961   —creator, producer, performer in "The Dick Van Dyke Show" on television, still running in syndication in 1978, awarded 11 Emmys, launched TV career of Mary Tyler Moore
1973   —producer, "The New Dick Van Dyke Show"
1978   —film producer, *Oh, God,* starring George Burns, John Denver

MEL BROOKS

1957   —co-author *Shinbone Alley* on Broadway
1963   —Academy Award for Best Short Subject, *The Critic*
1965   —television, creates "Get Smart" with Buck Henry
1968   —Academy Award for Best Screenplay, *The Producers*
1970   —film, *The Twelve Chairs*
1974   —film, *Blazing Saddles*
1975   —film, *Young Frankenstein*
1976   —film, *Silent Movie*
1978   —film, *High Anxiety*

BOB AND RAY

1920s

1922   —Raymond Walter Goulding born in Lowell, Massachusetts
1923   —Robert Bracket Elliot born in Boston, Massachusetts

1930s

———

1940s

1946   —first radio shows together, "Matinee with Bob and Ray,"
        "Break Fast with Bob and Ray"

1950s

1951   —first network contract, NBC
1952/57—win Peabody Awards for excellence in radio
1956   —albums, "Funtime," "Life of the Party"
1959   —CBS daily radio show

1960s

1961   —hiatus from radio appearances for one year
1962   —return to CBS radio
1966   —NBC-TV, "Today" Show—weekly appearances

1970s

1970   —Broadway show and tour of *Bob and Ray: The Two
        and Only*
1973–78—regular radio appearances, frequent TV appearances,
        "Tonight Show," etc., commercials, including American
        Express

ROWAN AND MARTIN

1920s

1922   —DICK MARTIN born in Battle Creek, Michigan
1922   —DAN HALE ROWAN born in Beggs, Oklahoma

1930s

———

1940s

———

1950s

1952 —first appearance as a team, Los Angeles
1958 —first film, *Once Upon a Horse*

1960s

1960 —first album, "Rowan & Martin at Work"
1967 —first TV, NBC special, "Rowan and Martin's Laugh In"
1968 —TV, NBC, "Laugh In" premieres as series—wins four
       Emmys
1969 —film, *The Maltese Bippy*

1970s

1973   —"Laugh In" goes off the air
1973–78—occasional concerts and TV specials
1978   —Dick Martin director/producer of "The Bob Newhart
        Show"
1978   —Dick Martin directs "The Waverly Wonders" starring
        Joe Namath
1978   —Dick Martin hosts "The Cheap Show"
1978   —Dan Rowan "semiretired" in Florida

STILLER AND MEARA

1920s

1928   —Jerry Stiller born in New York City

1930s

1933   —Anne Meara born in Long Island, New York

1940s

1950s

1954   —meet in New York and get married

1960s

1962   —become a team, Compass Players, Chicago
1967   —first album, "The Last Two People on Earth"
1969–78—various radio and TV commercials as a team

1970s

1971   —second album, "Laugh When You Like"
1975–76–Anne Meara, TV star of "Kate McShane"; co-star of "Rhoda"
1975–76–Jerry Stiller, TV star of "Joe and Sons"; film, *The Ritz*
1978   —TV, "Take 5" a series of five-minute comedy sketches

CLAIR AND MCMAHON

1920s

_____

1930s

1931(?)–Richard Clair Jones (DICK CLAIR) born in San Francisco, California
1933   —Mary Virginia Skinner (JENNA McMAHON) born in Kansas City, Missouri

1940s

_____

1950s

_____

1960s

1962   —meet at Cameo Playhouse, Los Angeles
1967   —first appearance as a team, the Purple Onion, San Francisco
1967–70–variety of TV and nightclub appearances

1970s

1971   —become sitcom writing team for Mary Tyler Moore
1972–78–permanent staff writers for the "Carol Burnett Show" 5 Emmy nominations, 2 Emmys
1978   —write TV special for Carol Burnett, "The Grass is Always Greener over the Septic Tank"

NICHOLS AND MAY

1920s
___

1930s
1931 —Michael Igor Peshkowsky (MIKE NICHOLS) born in Germany
1932 —Elaine Berlin (ELAINE MAY) born in Philadelphia, Pennsylvania

1940s
___

1950s
1952 —meet at the Compass Players, Chicago
1957 —move to New York
1959 —sellout performance at Town Hall, New York
1959 —first album, "Improvisations to Music"

1960s
1960 —Broadway show and album, "An Evening with Mike Nichols and Elaine May"
1961 —Broadway show closes, they split as a team
1962 —album, "Nichols and May Examine Doctors"
1965 —album, "The Best of Nichols and May"

1970s
___

The individual works of Mike Nichols and Elaine May

MIKE NICHOLS
1963 —Tony Award, Director, *Barefoot in the Park*
1964 —Director, *The Knack*, also *Luv* (Tony and New York Drama Critics awards)
1965 —Director, *The Odd Couple*, Tony Award
1966 —first film, director, *Who's Afraid of Virginia Woolf*

1967 —film, director, *The Graduate*, wins Academy Award
1971 —film, director, *Catch-22*
1974 —TV, writer, "Julie and Carol at Carnegie Hall," wins
       Emmy
1977 —TV, executive producer, "Family"
1978 —Director, *The Gin Game*
1978 —Producer, *Annie*, award winning Broadway musical

ELAINE MAY
1965 —film debut as actor in *Enter Laughing* by Carl Reiner
1969 —writer/director of one-act play, *Adaptation*
1971 —film, writer/director/co-star, *A New Leaf*
1972 —film, director, *The Heartbreak Kid*
1973 —film, director, *Mikey and Nicky*

BURNS AND SCHREIBER

1920s

———

1930s

1933 —John Francis Burns born in Boston, Massachusetts
1935 —Avery Schreiber born in Chicago, Illinois

1940s

———

1950s

1959–62—Burns teamed with George Carlin

1960s

1962 —Burns and Schreiber meet at the Second City, Chicago
1964 —first TV appearance as team, the "Jack Paar Show"
1967 —first album, "In One Head and Out the Other"
1967 —team breaks up

1972 —become team again
1973 —album, "Pure B.S."

1973   —ABC-TV special nominated for an Emmy
1973   —TV series, "Burns and Schreiber Comedy Hour"
1974   —final split as team
1975–78—Avery Schreiber—commercials, films, plays, etc.
1977   —Jack Burns, producer, "The Muppet Show"
1978   —Jack Burns, writer/producer *The Muppet Movie*

THE SMOTHERS BROTHERS

1920s

1930s

1937   —Thomas Bolyn Smothers III born in Governors Island,
         New York City
1938   —Richard Smothers born in Governors Island, New York
         City

1940s

1950s

1959   —debut at Purple Onion, San Francisco as folksingers
         (trio)

1960s

1960   —debut as duo, Aspen, Colorado
1961   —first comedy record album published (see below for
         complete list of titles)
1964   —TV, "Smothers Brothers Show," thirty-minute sitcom
1967–69—TV, CBS, "The Smothers Brothers Comedy Hour"
1969   —Tom Smothers produces the West Coast premiere of
         Hair

1970s

1970   —TV, ABC, "The Smothers Brothers Comedy Hour"
         (lasts three months only)
1971   —TV, syndicated series, "Smothers Brothers Organic
         Prime Time Space Ride"

24222 TWO FOR THE SHOW

1975   —TV, NBC, "Smothers Brothers Show" (brief)
1978   —Aladdin Hotel, Las Vegas, final appearance as a team
1978   —star on Broadway in *I Love My Wife* (do not play
        brothers)

Record albums of the Smothers Brothers

1961   —"The Songs and Comedy of The Smothers Brothers at
        the Purple Onion"
1962   —"The Two Sides of the Smothers Brothers"
1963   —"The Smothers Brothers 'Think Ethnic'"
1963   —"Curb Your Tongue, Knave"
1964   —"It Must Have Been Something I Said"
1964   —"Tour de Farce—American History and Other Unrelated
        Subjects"
1965   —"Aesop's Fables the Smothers Brothers Way"
1965   —"Mom Always Liked You Best"
1966   —"The Smothers Brothers Play It Straight"
1966   —"Golden Hits of the Smothers Brothers—Vol. 2" (there
        was no vol. 1)
1968   —"The Smothers Brothers Comedy Hour"

CHEECH AND CHONG

1920s

1930s

1939   —Thomas CHONG born in Alberta, Canada

1940s

1946   —Richard Marin (CHEECH) born in Los Angeles, Cali-
        fornia

1950s

1960s

1968   —in Canada, become a team
1969   —as a team, move to Los Angeles

1970s

1971   —first album, "Cheech and Chong"
1972   —second album, "Big Bambu," #1 Comedy Album of 1972
1973   —third album, "Los Cochinos," wins Grammy Award
1974   —fourth album, "Cheech and Chong's Wedding Album"
1978   —first film, *Up In Smoke*, released
1978   —fifth and sixth albums, "Up In Smoke" and "Sleeping Beauty"

The Marx Brothers—feature films

1929   —*The Cocoanuts*
1930   —*Animal Crackers*
1931   —*Monkey Business*
1932   —*Horse Feathers*
1933   —*Duck Soup*
1935   —*A Night at the Opera*
1937   —*A Day at the Races*
1938   —*Room Service*
1939   —*At the Circus*
1940   —*Go West*
1941   —*The Big Store*
1946   —*A Night in Casablanca*
1949   —*Love Happy*

Laurel and Hardy—feature films and selected short films

1926   —*Slipping Wives*, silent short
1926   —*Putting Pants on Philip*, silent short, first Laurel and Hardy film
1927   —*The Battle of the Century*, silent short
1928   —*Two Tars*, silent short
1929   —*Unaccustomed as We Are*, sound short
1929   —*Hollywood Review of 1929*, feature film, cameo appearance, sound

1931   —*Pardon Us*, first starring feature film (all films sound
           from now on)
1932   —*The Music Box*, film short, Academy Award winner
1932   —*Pack Up Your Troubles*, feature (all feature length films
           from now on)
1933   —*Fra Diavolo*
1933/34—*Sons of the Desert*
1934   —*Babes in Toyland*
1935   —*Bonnie Scotland*
1936   —*The Bohemian Girl*
           —*Our Relations*
1937   —*Way Out West*
           —*Pick a Star*
1938   —*Swiss Miss*
           —*Blockheads*
1939   —*The Flying Deuces*
1940   —*A Chump at Oxford*
           —*Saps at Sea*
1941   —*Great Guns*
1942   —*A-Haunting We Will Go*
1943   —*Jitterbugs*
           —*The Dancing Masters*
1944   —*The Big Noise*
           —*Nothing but Trouble*
1945   —*The Bullfighters*
1952   —*Atoll K* (also titled *Utopia*)

Abbott and Costello—feature films

1940   —*One Night in the Tropics*
1941   —*Buck Privates*
           —*In the Navy*
           —*Hold That Ghost*
           —*Keep 'Em Flying*
1942   —*Ride 'Em Cowboy*
           —*Rio Rita*
           —*Pardon My Sarong*
           —*Who Done It?*
           —*It Ain't Hay*
1943   —*Hit the Ice*

1944   —*In Society*
       —*Lost in a Harem*
1945   —*The Naughty Nineties*
       —*Abbott and Costello in Hollywood*
       —*Here Come the Coeds*
1946   —*Little Giant*
       —*Time of their Lives*
1947   —*Buck Privates Come Home*
       —*The Wistful Widow of Wagon Gap*
1948   —*The Noose Hangs High*
       —*Abbott and Costello Meet Frankenstein*
       —*Mexican Hayride*
1949   —*Abbott and Costello Meet the Killer, Boris Karloff*
1950   —*Abbott and Costello in the Foreign Legion*
1951   —*Abbott and Costello Meet the Invisible Man*
       —*Comin' Round the Mountain*
1952   —*Jack and the Beanstalk*
       —*Lost in Alaska*
       —*Abbott and Costello Meet Captain Kid*
1953   —*Abbott and Costello Go to Mars*
       —*Abbott and Costello Meet Jekyll and Hyde*
1955   —*Abbott and Costello Meet the Keystone Kops*
       —*Abbott and Costello Meet the Mummy*
1956   —*Dance with Me Henry*

COSTELLO BY HIMSELF
1959   —*The Thirty-Foot Bride of Candy Rock*

Burns and Allen—feature films

1932   —*The Big Broadcast*
1933   —*International House*
       —*College Humor*
1934   —*Six of a Kind*
       —*We're Not Dressing*
       —*Many Happy Returns*
1935   —*Love in Bloom*
       —*Here Comes Cookie*
       —*Big Broadcast of 1936*
1936   —*Big Broadcast of 1937*
       —*College Holiday*

1937   —A Damsel in Distress
1938   —College Swing
1939   —Honolulu

GRACIE ALONE
1939   —The Gracie Allen Murder Case
1941   —Mr. and Mrs. North
1944   —Two Girls and a Sailor

GEORGE ALONE
1975   —The Sunshine Boys
1978   —Oh, God
1978   —Sergeant Pepper's Lonely Hearts Club Band

The Three Stooges—feature films

1930   —Soup to Nuts
1933   —Turn Back the Clock
       —Meet the Baron
       —Dancing Lady
1934   —Fugitive Lovers
       —Hollywood Party
       —Gift of Gab
       —The Captain Hates the Sea
1938   —Start Cheering
1941   —Time Out for Rhythm
1942   —My Sister Eileen
1945   —Rockin' in the Rockies
1946   —Swing Parade of 1946
1951   —Gold Raiders
1959   —Have Rocket, Will Travel
1960   —Three Stooges Scrapbook (compilation)
       —Stop! Look! Laugh! (compilation)
1961   —Snow White and the Three Stooges
1962   —The Three Stooges Meet Hercules
       —The Three Stooges in Orbit
1963   —The Three Stooges Go Around the World in a Daze
       —It's a Mad Mad Mad Mad World
       —Four for Texas
1965   —The Outlaws Is Coming

MOE ALONE
1958   —*Space Master X-7*
1966   —*Don't Worry, We'll Think of a Title*

Martin and Lewis—feature films

1949   —*My Friend Irma*
1950   —*My Friend Irma Goes West*
        —*At War with the Army*
1951   —*That's My Boy*
        —*Sailor Beware*
1952   —*Jumping Jacks*
        —*Road to Bali* (guest stars)
1953   —*Scared Stiff*
        —*The Stooge*
        —*The Caddy*
        —*Money from Home*
1954   —*Living It Up*
        —*Three-Ring Circus*
1955   —*Artists and Models*
1956   —*Pardners*
        —*Hollywood or Bust*

Suggested Further Readings

This is a sparse list of books related to the subject matter. There are no volumes on the many teams after the demise of Martin and Lewis in the mid-fifties but the local library will lead you to articles and magazine pieces about the teams achieving prominence after 1956.

Burns, George. *Living it Up: or They Loved Me in Altoona.* NY: Putnam & Co., 1976.

* Elliott, Bob, and Goulding, Ray. *Write If You Get Work.* NY: Random House, 1975. (Many of Bob & Ray's best bits.)

* Firestone, Ross. *Breaking It Up: The Best Routines of the Stand-up Comics.* NY: Bantam Books, 1975.

Harmon, Jim. *The Great Radio Comedians.* NY: Doubleday and Co., 1970.

Manchel, Frank. *Yesterday's Clowns: The Rise of Film Comedy.* NY: Watts Publishing Co., 1973.

* Maltin, Leonard. *Movie Comedy Teams.* NY: The New American Library, Inc., 1970.

Marx, Arthur. *Everybody Loves Somebody Sometimes.* NY: Hawthorne Books, 1974. (Martin & Lewis.)

Mast, Gerald. *The Comic Mind.* Indianapolis/IND: Bobbs-Merrill & Co., 1973.

* McCabe, John. *Mr. Laurel and Mr. Hardy.* NY: The New American Library, Inc., 1968.

* Mulholland, Jim. *The Abbott and Costello Book.* NY: Popular Library, 1975.

Smith, Bill. *The Vaudevillians.* NY: Macmillan Publishing Co., Inc., 1976.

Wilde, Larry. *The Great Comedians.* Secaucus/NJ: Citadel Press, 1973.

* Wolf, William. *The Marx Brothers.* NY: Pyramid Publications, 1975.

* paperback

Index

About the Author

Lonnie Burr began his long association with comedy by making a nifty twenty-five bucks for a Policeman's Benefit at the Pasadena Civic Auditorium. He was only five and ostensibly did a vaudeville turn as a song-and-dance man. After being told vaudeville was dead, Lonnie gingerly advanced his career to other areas and played Lon McAllister's son in the film "Yank In Korea;" a running role in the 1950 TV series, "The Ruggles" starring Charlie Ruggles; and a lead at the Pasadena Playhouse. He was six by then and moved on to other films, TV shows, commercials, and a lead in a radio soap. In 1955 he was signed by the Disney Studios as one of the four male Mouseketeers that survived intact for the run of "The Mickey Mouse Club." Undaunted but perturbed by the latter experience, he left show business and got an M.A. in Theatre from the University of California at Los Angeles. Later he returned to performing and made numerous pictures and TV shows, as well as performing in Broadway and off-Broadway musicals and dramas.

As a writer, Lonnie is currently contributing editor on *Footlights Magazine* and has written satire, reviews, and articles for such journals as *The Village Voice, the LA Times Calendar* and *American Film Magazine*. (His poetry is consistently published in poetry quarterlies and has won a number of awards.) Lonnie's play, "Occam's Razor," was done at Manhattan Theatre Club in New York City and Callboard Theatre in Los Angeles, and his two–act comedy "Over The Hill" was produced last year at the MET Theatre in Hollywood. He has just finished another drama, "Children Are Strangers," and is currently working on a novel about show business.